THE LAW OF MEDICAL MALPRACTICE

2nd Edition

by
Margaret C. Jasper

Oceana's Legal Almanac Series
Law for the Layperson

2001
Oceana Publications, Inc.
Dobbs Ferry, New York

Information contained in this work has been obtained by Oceana Publications from sources believed to be reliable. However, neither the Publisher nor its authors guarantee the accuracy or completeness of any information published herein, and neither Oceana nor its authors shall be responsible for any errors, omissions or damages arising from the use of this information. This work is published with the understanding that Oceana and its authors are supplying information, but are not attempting to render legal or other professional services. If such services are required, the assistance of an appropriate professional should be sought.

Library of Congress Control Number: 2001135864

ISBN: 0-379-11359-7

Oceana's Legal Almanac Series: Law for the Layperson
ISSN 1075-7376

©2001 by Oceana Publications, Inc.

To My Husband Chris

Your love and support
are my motivation and inspiration

-and-

In memory of my son, Jimmy

Table of Contents

CHAPTER 2:
THEORIES OF LIABILITY AND ELEMENTS OF PROOF

CHAPTER 3:
RESPONSIBLE PARTIES AND THEIR DEFENSES

CHAPTER 4:
DAMAGES

CHAPTER 5:
HOSPITAL LIABILITY

CHAPTER 6:
MEDICAL RECORDS

CHAPTER 7:
MEDICAL MALPRACTICE LITIGATION

APPENDICES

ABOUT THE AUTHOR

MARGARET C. JASPER is an attorney engaged in the general practice of law in South Salem, New York, concentrating in the areas of personal injury and entertainment law. Ms. Jasper holds a Juris Doctor degree from Pace University School of Law, White Plains, New York, is a member of the New York and Connecticut bars, and is certified to practice before the United States District Courts for the Southern and Eastern Districts of New York, the United States Court of Appeals for the Second Circuit, and the United States Supreme Court.

Ms. Jasper has been appointed to the panel of arbitrators of the American Arbitration Association and the law guardian panel for the Family Court of the State of New York, is a member of the Association of Trial Lawyers of America, and is a New York State licensed real estate broker and member of the Westchester County Board of Realtors, operating as Jasper Real Estate, in South Salem, New York. Margaret Jasper maintains a website at http://members.aol.com/JasperLaw.

Ms. Jasper is the author and general editor of the following legal almanacs: Juvenile Justice and Children's Law; Marriage and Divorce; Estate Planning; The Law of Contracts; The Law of Dispute Resolution; Law for the Small Business Owner; The Law of Personal Injury; Real Estate Law for the Homeowner and Broker; Everyday Legal Forms; Dictionary of Selected Legal Terms; The Law of Medical Malpractice; The Law of Product Liability; The Law of No-Fault Insurance; The Law of Immigration; The Law of Libel and Slander; The Law of Buying and Selling; Elder Law; The Right to Die; AIDS Law; The Law of Obscenity and Pornography; The Law of Child Custody; The Law of Debt Collection; Consumer Rights Law; Bankruptcy Law for the Individual Debtor; Victim's Rights Law; Animal Rights Law; Workers' Compensation Law; Employee Rights in the Workplace; Probate Law; Environmental Law; Labor Law; The Americans with Disabilities Act; The Law of Capital Punishment; Education Law; The Law of Violence Against Women; Landlord-Tenant Law; Insurance Law; Religion and the Law; Commercial Law; Motor Vehicle Law; Social Security Law; The Law of Drunk Driving; The Law of Speech and the First Amendment; Employment Discrimination Under Title VII; Hospital Liability Law; Home Mortgage Law Primer; Copyright Law; Patent Law; Trademark Law; Special Education Law; The Law of Attachment and Garnishment; Banks and their Customers; and Credit Cards and the Law.

INTRODUCTION

This legal almanac explores the area of law known generally as "medical malpractice." There are three parties who have an interest in medical malpractice litigation. The two most obvious parties are the injured patient who is seeking recompense for suffering he would not have otherwise endured; and the physician or other health care provider responsible for causing the injury, who is now being sued and at risk of having a financially devastating judgment rendered against him or her.

The third party with an interest in medical malpractice litigation is society, which bears a financial burden as a result of the increasing medical costs and insurance premiums caused by such litigation; and experiences a less trusting and open relationship with their medical providers, who are being more and more careful and conservative in their practices so as to avoid such litigation.

This almanac sets forth the elements necessary to prove the various theories of liability which support a prima facie medical malpractice claim, the defenses to such claims, the litigation procedures unique to medical malpractice, the responsible parties and apportionment of liability, and the damages recoverable. The reader is cautioned, however, when researching a particular problem, not to rely on a general discussion of the law, but to always check the law of their own jurisdictions.

This almanac also discusses ways in which an individual can investigate the background and credentials of prospective health care providers to try and protect themselves from being victims of medical malpractice.

The Appendix provides sample documents, applicable statutes, resource information, medical terminology and other pertinent information and data. The Glossary contains definitions of many of the terms used throughout the almanac.

CHAPTER 1:
PROTECTING YOURSELF FROM MEDICAL MISTAKES

IN GENERAL

Historically, patients have relied on the advice of their medical providers with few, if any, questions asked. It was assumed that the doctor was the expert and knew what was best for the patient. Although the majority of health care providers are competent professionals with the utmost concern for the well-being of their patients, medical mistakes do occur. And, unfortunately, due to the negligence of a minority of health care providers, the medical profession has come under attack as accounts of horrendous medical mistakes have been reported to the public.

Nevertheless, not every medical mistake qualifies as actionable medical malpractice. Medical malpractice involves the commission of a tort—a wrongful act—as do all personal injury actions. However, there exist a number of differences unique to medical malpractice litigation, and the standards of proof are much higher than in a simple negligence case.

In addition, largely due to the power and support behind the health care industry, lawyers for this powerful industry have been successful in passing legislation designed to reduce medical malpractice litigation. Such legislation includes shortened statutes of limitations in medical malpractice cases, limits on damage awards, and the placement of caps on legal fees in an effort to dissuade lawyers from taking on such cases. Some states require the lawyer to prove the merits of a case even before the action can be filed.

Unfortunately, such restrictive legislation does nothing to reduce medical malpractice and promote patient safety. Thus, the primary incentive for improving the quality of health care is through successful medical malpractice litigation and large monetary awards. In the meantime, the public must be made aware of the ways they can try and protect themselves from medical negligence before it occurs.

STATISTICS

Unfortunately, recent statistics demonstrate that between 44,000 and 88,000 hospital patients die each year as a result of medical negligence. Further, this figure does not include malpractice-related deaths which occur outside the hospital setting.

The Association for Responsible Medicine (ARM), an entity concerned with preventing and exposing medical negligence, has gathered some startling statistics about medical malpractice:

1. Over one million hospital patients will suffer an injury as the result of an a medical mistake.

2. More than 180,000 die partly as the result of a medical mistake according to the Harvard Medical Practice Study.

3. No government agency—state or Federal—maintains a record of this epidemic.

4. Studies show that medical malpractice is more likely if a doctor has made mistakes in the past.

5. Doctors with many malpractice settlements are allowed to retain their licenses and hospital privileges.

6. Doctors are not required to carry liability insurance to cover patients injured by a medical mistake.

7. Doctors may perform surgery that was not authorized because of medical consent laws that protect doctors.

8. A doctor may allow another person to perform surgery without the patient's consent.

9. At some hospitals, 18% to 36% of patients may suffer from a medical mistake that causes injury or death.

10. Medical mistakes usually go unreported.

11. State laws generally prohibit the release of a hospital report on a medical mistake even to the injured patient or his/her family.

INVESTIGATING THE CREDENTIALS OF A HEALTH CARE PROVIDER

No matter what the cause may be for what appears to be a growing problem, it is crucial that individuals learn ways in which to try and protect themselves from medical mistakes. Fortunately, the average consumer today has many more ways to do so. For example, the internet provides the consumer with a wealth of resources and information concerning prospective health care providers that was never available so easily in the past.

The American Medical Association provides background and credentialing information on physicians at its website [http://www.ama-assn.org]. You can find out where your prospective doctor went to medical school, whether or not they are board-certified, as well as their office address and phone number. The American Board of Medical Specialties operates a website [http://www.abms.org/] where you can find out if a specific physician has been certified as a specialist by one of their specialty boards.

In addition, the Federation of State Medical Boards operates a website [http://www.fsmb.org] which has direct links to all of the state medical licensing boards. You can access your state's medical board to find out the status of a doctor's license and whether he or she has ever been the subject of disciplinary procedures. Several states now also include medical malpractice and hospital disciplinary action information on their own websites.

Another service which provides comprehensive background information on health care providers nationwide is Knowx [http://www.knowx.com]. For a relatively small fee, the consumer can access information concerning a health care provider's location, credentials, license verification and disciplinary actions. The Knowx "searchpointe" service includes information on medical doctors (MDs), doctors of osteopathy (DOs) and doctors of chiropractic (DCs) with active licenses to practice in the United States. Knowx also contains a database which lists court information, enabling the consumer to find out whether any lawsuits or judgments have been filed against a particular doctor.

The County Clerk in a particular jurisdiction generally provides public access to its database of legal actions filed in the jurisdiction. It is possible to research whether a particular doctor has been the subject of any lawsuits, and even review copies of the litigation papers, such as the actual complaint, which are on file with the Clerk's office.

There are also companies who specialize in checking the background of health care providers. Health Care Choices is a New York not-for-profit corporation dedicated to educating the public about the nation's health care system. HealthGrades.com, Inc. is a private company that provides "report cards" on doctors, hospitals, health plans and nursing homes.

Profiling Laws

In an effort to improve access to information concerning the credentials of health care providers, a number of states have passed profiling laws. Some states, such as California and Massachusetts, provide malpractice information to the public as a result of a requirement included in profiling legislation. Profiling laws require state agencies to compile practice information on physicians and other practitioners from various sources and then publish the resulting profile on the internet. Profiles generally include information such as the practitioner's education and training, specialty, hospital affiliations, disciplinary actions, closed malpractice cases and hospital disciplinary proceedings.

There is variation among states with respect to penalties imposed on practitioners for failing to report or for reporting inaccurate information. For example, Idaho assesses a $50/day fine for the period a practitioner is not in compliance with the statutory reporting requirements. In Florida, failure to comply with the profiling statute can subject the practitioner to disciplinary action including failure to have a license renewed.

A Directory of State Physician Licensing Bureaus is set forth at Appendix 1.

RESEARCHING A HOSPITAL'S CREDENTIALS

Hospitalization is a serious matter. However, all to often, consumers do not look into the background of the hospital they are preparing to enter. It is critical that the consumer investigate the hospital which will be responsible for their care while undergoing a medical procedure. There is much information readily available to the consumer who requests it.

For example, hospitals are required by law to maintain a statistical record on all procedures. The consumer can request this information. Also, the consumer may inquire about the credentials of the hospital's staff, including their nurses and others associated with the prospective patient's daily care. The prospective patient should familiarize themselves with the hospital's "Patient Bill of Rights," which lists the patient's rights in reference to many aspects of care, such as confidentiality, safety, access to care, communications, hospital rules and regulations.

A Directory of State Licensing Agencies for Medical Facilities is set forth at Appendix 2.

The Joint Commission on Accreditation of Healthcare Organizations (JCAHO)

The Joint Commission on Accreditation of Healthcare Organizations (JCAHO) is the nation's predominant standards-setting and accrediting body in health care and evaluates and accredits nearly 19,000 health care organizations and programs in the United States. The JCAHO was founded in 1951 as an independent, not-for-profit organization. The mission of the JCAHO is to continuously improve the safety and quality of care provided to the public through the provision of health care accreditation and related services that support performance improvement in health care organizations. The JCAHO also sponsors a variety of education programs and provides relevant publications for health care professionals.

The JCAHO evaluation and accreditation services are provided for the following types of organizations:

1. General, psychiatric, children's and rehabilitation hospitals.

2. Health care networks, including health plans, integrated delivery networks and preferred provider organizations.

3. Home care organizations, including those that provide home health services, personal care and support services, home infusion and other pharmacy services, durable medical equipment services and hospice services.

4. Nursing homes and other long term care facilities, including subacute care programs, dementia programs and long term care pharmacies.

5. Assisted Living residencies that provide or coordinate personal services, 24-hour supervision and assistance, activities and health-related services.

6. Behavioral health care organizations, including those that provide mental health, chemical dependency, and mental retardation/developmental disabilities services for patients of various ages in various organized service settings; and managed behavioral health care organizations.

7. Ambulatory care providers, including outpatient surgery facilities, rehabilitation centers, infusion centers, group practices and others.

8. Clinical laboratories.

Accreditation by the JCAHO is recognized nationwide as a symbol of quality that indicates that an organization meets certain performance standards. The JCAHO's standards address the organization's level of performance in key functional areas, such as patient rights. The JCAHO develops its standards in consultation with health care experts, providers, measurement experts, purchasers and consumers. To earn and maintain accreditation, an organization must undergo an on-site survey by a JCAHO survey team at least every three years. Laboratories must be surveyed every two years.

The JCAHO is governed by a 28-member Board of Commissioners, which includes nurses, physicians, consumers, medical directors, administrators, providers, employers, labor representatives, health plan leaders, quality experts, ethicists, health insurance administrators and educators. Its corporate members are the American College of Physicians; the American College of Surgeons; the American Dental Association; the American Hospital Association; and the American Medical Association. More than 650 physicians, nurses, health care administrators, medical technologists, psychologists, respiratory therapists, pharmacists, durable medical equipment providers and social workers are employed by the JCAHO to conduct accreditation surveys.

JCAHO Quality Check

The JCAHO publishes "Quality Check"—a comprehensive internet guide to accredited organizations, where a consumer can search for quality information on their local hospital. Quality Check provides a list of nearly 20,000 JCAHO-accredited health care organizations and programs throughout the United States and includes each organization's name, address, telephone number, accreditation decision, accreditation date, and current accreditation status and effective date. In addition, for more in-depth quality information, consumers can check the individual performance reports available for many accredited organizations. Performance reports provide detailed information about an organization's performance and how it compares to similar organizations.

JCAHO Five Steps to Safer Health Care

The JCAHO has recommended the following five steps to obtaining safer health care:

Step One: Ask Questions

The patient is advised to speak freely with their medical provider if they have any concerns. It is okay to ask questions and to expect answers you can understand. Thus, it is important to choose a doctor whom you feel comfortable talking to about your health and treatment. In addition, it is advisable to take a relative or friend with you if this will assist you in asking questions and understanding the answers.

Step Two: Medications

It is important to keep a list of all medicines you take and to advise both your medical providers and pharmacist about all the medicines you take, including over-the-counter medicines such as aspirin, ibuprofen, vitamins and herbals. You should also advise your medical providers and pharmacist about any drug allergies you may have.

When you are given a prescription, ask the pharmacist about side effects and what foods or other things to avoid while taking the medication. Be sure to read the label, including warnings, and make sure you know how to properly administer the medication. Make sure the medication you receive is the medication your doctor ordered for you. If the medication looks different than you expected, ask the pharmacist about the difference, if any.

Step Three: Obtaining Test Results

Make sure you get the results of all tests and procedures performed. If you have any questions, ask the doctor or nurse when and how you will obtain the results. Further, don't assume the results are fine if you don't get them when expected. Follow up and call the doctor. If you have any questions about what the test results mean, ask for an explanation.

Step Four: Choosing a Hospital

If you need hospital care, talk with your doctor about your care options. You should verify which hospitals are accepted by your insurance, HMO or PPO plan. If you have more than one hospital to choose from, ask the doctor which hospital has the best care for your condition and ask him or her to explain the advantages or special characteristics of each hospital where he or she practices Hospitals do a good job of treating a wide range of problems. For some procedures, however, such as heart bypass surgery, research shows results are often better at hospitals doing a lot of these procedures. Also, you can research your local hospital by consulting JCAHO'S Quality Check on the internet, as further described above.

Some of the questions and concerns the JCAHO recommends a patient inquire about before choosing a hospital include:

1. Is the hospital conveniently located? Can you and your family get there easily for scheduled as well as emergency medical care?

2. Is the hospital accredited by a nationally recognized accrediting body, such as the JCAHO?

3. Does the hospital have a written description of its services and fees and what resources, if any, the hospital provides to help you find financial assistance if you need it?

5. Is the hospital clean? Visit the hospital and look around. Ask to see the waiting rooms and patient care rooms. Does the waiting room look comfortable? Would you want to recuperate in the patient rooms? Do the patient rooms have comfortable chairs for visitors? Do you have privacy in the room?

6. Do the services and specialties provided by the hospital meet your specific medical needs? Do you have a medical condition requiring specialized attention?

7. What is the hospital's success record in carrying out the specific medical procedure you need and how often is the particular procedure done?

8. What is the specific training of the physician who will perform the procedure?

9. Ask to see a copy of the hospital's patient rights and responsibilities information.

10. Who will be responsible for maintaining your personal care plan and how will you and/or your family be kept up-to-date on your medical care?

11. Does the hospital have social workers and what services do the social workers provide? For example, social workers usually help patients and their families find emotional, social, clinical, physical and financial support services.

12. Will a discharge plan be developed for you before you leave the hospital and will the hospital provide you with the necessary training to continue your care in your home after you have been discharged?

Step Five: Surgery

Make sure you understand what will happen if you need surgery. You, your doctor and surgeon should all agree on exactly what will be done during the operation. Ask how long the surgery will take, what will happen after the surgery and how you will feel during your recovery. Ask who will be in charge of your care while you are in the hospital. Advise the surgeon, anesthesiologist and nurses if you have allergies or have ever had a bad reaction to anesthesia. Before you leave the hospital, ask about follow-up care and understand all instructions.

More information about the JCAHO may be found on its website located at http://www.jcaho.org/ or by calling its Customer Service Center at (630) 792-5800.

GETTING A SECOND OPINION

When faced with the decision about whether to submit to a particular medical procedure or treatment, it is wise for the patient to obtain a second opinion from a physician not affiliated with the primary physician. It is also important to make sure that the intended procedure is FDA-approved. Surgeries without FDA approval are considered experimental and results therefore are uncertain.

EMERGENCY CARE

The information above is designed to assist the prospective patient in investigating a hospital in anticipation of a planned medical procedure or treatment. However, oftentimes, an individual finds themselves in the midst of an unexpected health crisis requiring the emergency admission to a hospital. Nevertheless, one can also prepare themselves for such an unanticipated event.

For example, individuals should keep a medical journal which sets forth important health-related information, such as: (a) any allergies they have to medications or foods and the anticipated reaction; (b) an outline of past hospitalizations, surgeries and significant medical conditions and treatments; (c) current medical problems, if any; (d) a list of prescription drugs being taken along with the instructions concerning dosage; (e) a list of over-the-counter medications being taken along with information on the purpose and frequency of the medications being taken; (f) periodic height, weight and blood pressure measurements; (g) insurance information; and (h) any other information related to the individual's health.

In addition, as discussed below, one should execute advanced directives and health care appointments and provide copies to their health care provider, attorney, and family members.

ADVANCE DIRECTIVES

Living Will and Durable Power of Attorney for Health Care Organizations (JCAHO)

An individual executes a Living Will to formalize their right to refuse life support or other medical treatment in advance in the event of a sudden illness or injury. The document may specify the treatment that may or may not be used. For example, the administration of oxygen may be approved, but more extraordinary methods of life support may be expressly prohibited.

The document must be executed by an individual, over the age of majority, at a time when the individual is mentally competent. The Durable Power of Attorney for Health Care appoints an attorney-in-fact to make the health care decisions in accordance with the individual's wishes as expressed in the living will or other health care declaration.

Where the individual's wishes are not expressed in the document or any other health care declaration, or otherwise conveyed to the attorney-in-fact, he or she is obligated to act in the individual's best interests. Nevertheless, if the individual is still competent to make his or her own health care decisions, those decisions will prevail over those of the attorney-in-fact, even if they contradict the express provisions of the living will or durable power of attorney.

Upon admission to the hospital, it is important that a patient, or the patient's representative, advise the hospital staff and the attending physician of the existence of the patient's Living Will and Durable Power of Attorney for Health Care, and provide a copy, so that the patient's wishes will be carried out in the event the patient's condition deteriorates to the point that he or she is unable to express his or her wishes. Every hospital is required by federal law to give the patient some form of advance directives and medical surrogate designation form.

In situations where the patient is incompetent, has not executed a living will and durable power of attorney, and has no known relatives, the health care provider should apply to the court for an order concerning proposed treatments or the withholding of such treatments. In such a case, the court may appoint a conservator to make such decisions.

A sample Durable Power of Attorney for Health Care is set forth at Appendix 3.

Release from Liability

Most hospitals will require a patient, or his or her representative, to sign a document which releases the attending physician, the hospital and its employees from liability if treatment is withheld or withdrawn. The document generally states the circumstances of the patient's condition, e.g., brain death, etc., giving rise to the request to terminate treatment.

The release of liability document also references the patient's living will and durable power of attorney for health care as proof of the patient's desire to forego life sustaining procedures and his or her appointment of an agent to make this decision if he or she is unable to do so.

In a subsequent medical malpractice action, a defendant may set forth a defense alleging that the patient assumed the risk of non-treatment by virtue of the release of liability. However, the release would not limit the health care provider's liability for negligence. If the release contained such a provision, it would likely be unenforceable on public policy grounds.

A sample Release from Liability is set forth at Appendix 4.

A Patient's Right to Refuse Treatment

The Competent Adult

Most states acknowledge that a competent adult has the legal right to refuse medical care. On the other hand, many states also set forth certain policy concerns—such as preservation of life and suicide prevention—to limit this right.

The courts have looked to the circumstances concerning the patient when denial of the patient's rights are put in issue. Generally, if the patient is capable of recovery, the state's interest in preserving life has more merit then when the patient is on his or her death bed with no possibility of recovery. Further, the courts have distinguished between the act of suicide and the patient's right to die a natural death without being placed on life support.

States have also expressed concern over the impact refusal of medical treatment will have on innocent third parties—in particular, minor children. For example, if the refusal to have a critical blood transfusion will cause a single mother to die and leave her children orphaned, the court will likely order the parent to undergo the treatment. The court will also usually order a pregnant woman to undergo treatment which is necessary to protect the unborn child.

A health care provider—e.g., on moral grounds—may not be able to accept the patient's wishes to forego necessary treatment. In that case, the health care provider should assist the patient in locating a health care provider who is able to care for the patient according to his or her wishes. Some health care providers have raised concerns that withholding treatment is tantamount to abandonment. However, the courts have generally held that where treatment would be futile, terminating or withholding treatment is not abandonment.

Minors

Minors are incompetent to make decisions concerning their right to forego medical treatment. Thus, the minor's parents make the decisions on the minor's behalf. However, when a minor is in critical need of treatment but the parent—e.g., due to religious beliefs—will not consent, court orders are routinely granted to the health care provider to administer the treatment. In some cases, a guardian is appointed by the court to protect the child.

A health care provider who is faced with a life-threatening situation must render the necessary treatment to the minor despite the parent's wishes, and instruct the parents to obtain a court order immediately if they want to prevent such treatment.

In situations where the minor is in such a physical state that any attempt to sustain life would be futile and cruel, the courts have held that the parents and health care provider can mutually decide to withhold treatment without seeking a court order. Nevertheless, this law generally does not permit the withholding of food and water as a means to hasten death in the case of a minor.

Religious Beliefs

Certain religious groups hold that medical treatment—e.g., blood transfusions—violates their religious beliefs. In these cases, the courts have generally held that a competent adult, without dependent children, may refuse treatment. However, as previously discussed, where there is an overriding state concern, such as the protection of third parties, the adult may be compelled to accept the treatment.

CHAPTER 2:
THEORIES OF LIABILITY AND ELEMENTS OF PROOF

MEDICAL NEGLIGENCE

Negligence is the predominant theory of medical malpractice litigation. In order to recover in a medical malpractice action, the plaintiff must establish the following elements:

(1) The existence of the health care provider's duty to the plaintiff—i.e., the health care provider/patient relationship;

(2) The applicable standard of care and the health care provider's violation of that standard—i.e., the breach of duty;

(3) A causal connection between the health care provider's violation of the standard of care and the harm suffered; and

(4) A compensable injury—i.e., damages.

The Health Care Provider/Patient Relationship

Liability for medical malpractice cannot exist unless there is a health care provider/patient relationship which creates a duty on the part of the health care provider to render acceptable medical care to the patient. The health care provider/patient relationship is generally found to exist where the health care provider undertakes to treat the patient, thus creating a professional relationship.

The health care provider/patient relationship may also be based on a contract theory, in that the patient pays, or agrees to pay, the health care provider for his or her services.

Once the health care provider/patient relationship is deemed to have arisen, it cannot be unilaterally terminated by the health care provider without there being a mutual understanding by both health care provider and patient or the health care provider may be held liable for abandonment of the patient.

Termination of the relationship may result when:

1. The patient terminates the relationship; or

2. The treatment undertaken is completed and further treatment is no longer necessary; or

3. The health care provider notifies the patient that he or she can no longer render services to the patient and either (a) refers the patient to another health care provider, or (b) extends a reasonable amount of time for the patient to find other suitable medical care.

The Standard of Care

The basic theory of medical malpractice involves a finding of fault on the part of the health care provider in that his or her conduct fell below a socially acceptable standard of medical care. Thus, without proof that the health care provider failed to exercise the required level of care, even when the treatment or procedure caused an injury or produced less than desirable results, the plaintiff would not win the case.

The burden of proving that the health care provider's medical care fell below acceptable standards rests with the plaintiff. The proof is usually necessarily demonstrated by the use of expert testimony, i.e., other health care providers qualified in the particular area of medicine, who review the case and render an opinion that the defendant health care provider rendered negligent care.

As set forth in Section 299A of the Restatement of Torts, the standard of care is not that of the most highly skilled member of the profession, nor is it that of the average member of the profession, but it is the standard of care that is common to those who are recognized in the profession itself as qualified and competent to engage in it.

For example, if the care rendered by the most highly skilled surgeon was used as the measuring stick for negligence, then the majority of surgeons would automatically be found liable.

Further, a health care provider's skill may fall below the average member of the profession, yet the health care provider may still be deemed qualified and competent.

A Causal Connection

The final requirement to establish a prima facie medical malpractice case is to demonstrate that there was a causal connection between the health care provider's violation of the standard of care and the harm suffered. The plaintiff will lose the case even if it is proven that there was a violation of the standard of care, if there is no causal connection established.

To determine causation, there are two common tests:

1. The "but for" test—If it can be proven that it was more probably true than not, that the patient's injury would not have occurred "but for" the defendant's actions, causation has been established under this test.

2. The "substantial factor" test—If it can be proven that the defendant's actions were a substantial factor in bringing about the injury, causation has been established under this test.

Res Ipsa Loquitur

Some states permit the doctrine of res ipsa loquitur in medical malpractice actions as a means of shifting the burden of proof to the defendant. Under this doctrine, the plaintiff must submit evidence that the injury would not have occurred in the absence of negligence. The elements of the doctrine of res ipsa loquitur are:

1. The injury does not normally occur in the absence of negligence;

2. The health care provider had exclusive control of the instrumentality or agency of the injury; and

3. The injuries were not caused by the plaintiff's own contributory fault.

If the plaintiff was under the exclusive control and care of more than one health care provider, then all such persons would be named as defendants in the action. This places pressure on each individual to place the blame where it is due to avoid his or her own liability.

A Compensable Injury

Another requirement for the plaintiff to prevail in a medical malpractice action is that the plaintiff must have sustained a compensable injury. If the plaintiff is able to establish the health care provider/patient relationship, and that there was a violation of the standard of care, the plaintiff is still not entitled to damages if he or she did not sustain a compensable injury as a result of the violation.

OTHER THEORIES OF LIABILITY

Negligent Prescription of Medications and Medical Devices

If a medical malpractice case involves injuries sustained as a result of a particular drug, the pharmaceutical manufacturer may be joined as a defendant. In most cases, however, the manufacturer will not be liable unless they failed to warn of certain hazards related to the drug. More commonly, the physician will have ignored the manufacturer's instructions or will have prescribed an incorrect medication or dosage, which resulted in the plaintiff's injuries.

Physicians, as "learned intermediaries," have a duty to advise the patient of all of the risks and side effects of medications or medical devices the physician prescribes. This ensures that the patient is able to make an informed decision about whether they will take the medication or utilize the particular medical device. If the physician fails to advise the patient of the manufacturer's warning, or otherwise neglects the warnings provided by the manufacturer, the physician is negligent and will be liable for any resulting injuries to the patient.

For example, if a pharmaceutical manufacturer adequately informs a physician that a particular drug is not suitable for children, and the physician ignores this warning and prescribes the medication for a child, the physician will be liable to the patient for any injuries which may occur as a result of the drug.

The physician's duty stems from his or her superior medical knowledge. It is presumed that the physician knows that the patient relies on the physician's knowledge and judgment. As a learned intermediary, it is also presumed that the physician, who has been given adequate information concerning a particular medication, is in the best position to know whether that medication should be prescribed for a particular patient.

If a physician is not familiar with particular medication, prior to prescribing the drug, they will generally consult the Physicians' Desk Reference (PDR) for detailed information about the drug, its side effects, and interactions with other drugs. In the PDR, the doctor can learn everything necessary for the safe use of a drug.

Limited Liability of Pharmaceutical Manufacturer

In the case of prescription drugs, the pharmaceutical manufacturer's duty is to the physician, as a "learned intermediary," instead of to the consumer directly. Thus, the manufacturer's liability is limited provided it properly and adequately informs the physician of all of the risks associated with the particular drug. If the pharmaceutical manufacturer fails to adequately warn the physician, an otherwise safe drug becomes unreasonably dangerous due to the manufacturer's failure to warn.

Relying on the "learned intermediary" role of the physician, the pharmaceutical company only owes a duty to the consumer to ensure that the medications they manufacture and sell are reasonably safe when used by the consumer as intended. To make sure that the drug is safe, the manufacturer must properly research the drug's possible side effects and risks before putting it on the market. Although a particular drug may have been given FDA approval, this does not guarantee that the product is safe.

If a patient suffers injuries as a result of a particular medication, he or she can bring a lawsuit against the drug manufacturer under all of the usual product liability theories—e.g., strict liability, negligence, and breach of warranty, if the manufacturer was to blame. However, if it is the physician's conduct which is at fault for not heeding the warnings and information provided by the manufacturer, then the physician may be sued for medical negligence in a medical malpractice lawsuit.

Lack of Informed Consent/Unauthorized Treatment

An individual has an absolute right to prevent an unauthorized contact with his or her person. Lack of informed consent is a type of negligence which occurs when the health care provider fails to obtain the patient's consent prior to a surgical procedure or course of treatment, or fails to adequately inform the patient of all of the risks associated with the particular treatment.

Lack of informed consent means that the patient did not fully understand what the health care provider was going to do, and was injured as a result of the health care provider's action. Further, the patient claims that if he had known what the health care provider planned to do, the patient would not have consented and, therefore, would have avoided the injury.

Further, treatment of the patient without the requisite consent may lead to a cause of action for battery—an intentional tort. Prior to performing any type of invasive procedure or non-customary treatment, the health care provider is obligated to obtain the patient's informed consent. If the health care provider does not obtain such consent, any treatment rendered is deemed unauthorized and the health care provider will be liable to the patient for any negative consequences.

Absent an emergency, if the health care provider is able to ascertain, in advance of a surgical procedure, all of the possible alternatives available if an unexpected situation should arise during the operation, the patient should be informed of the alternatives and given the chance to decide if those alternatives are acceptable before the health care provider proceeds with the procedure.

A table of possible complications associated with common medical procedures is set forth at Appendix 5.

A patient gives consent to medical treatment either by (1) express consent or (2) implied consent.

Express Consent

Express consent is obtained either in writing or orally. The health care provider is required to fully disclose all of the known and significant facts relevant to the procedure, in layperson's language, so that the patient can make an intelligent decision as to whether to go forward with the treatment. The following information should be provided to the patient to satisfy the informed consent requirement:

1. The diagnosis of the patient's condition and the prognosis without the proposed treatment;

2. The nature of the proposed treatment;

3. The goal to be achieved by the proposed treatment and the chance that the treatment will be successful;

4. The risks of the proposed treatment;

5. Any alternative treatments to the proposed treatment;

6. Identify:

> (a) The health care provider(s) who discussed the proposed treatment with the patient;

> (b) The health care provider(s) who will perform the proposed treatment;

7. Obtain consent to deviate from the proposed treatment in case of unforeseen circumstances.

8. Obtain consent to dispose of any tissue, organs or other body parts, if needed, for pathological study or research;

9. Acknowledgment that the patient's questions were fully discussed and adequately answered.

10. The patient's and/or legal guardian's signature, the signature of a witness, and the date, time, and location that the consent form was signed. If the patient is a minor, the parents may consent to the procedure, or, in the case of divorce, it is usually the parent having legal custody who may consent.

Where the health care provider has failed to obtain such consent, or where the quality of the consent is challenged, the patient may claim lack of informed consent for the procedure.

A sample Informed Consent Agreement is set forth at Appendix 6.

Implied Consent

Implied consent is obtained, for example, when a patient submits to a relatively simple procedure. However, there is no implied consent where the procedure is invasive or non-customary.

Further, once a surgeon begins an internal surgical procedure, there is a presumption of implied consent if the surgeon does other "necessary" procedures in the process. This is so even if there are relatives in the vicinity because the surgeon is not permitted to leave the operating room, once the surgery has begun, to obtain consent.

However, such implied consent only applies to necessary procedures. If the procedure is elective, the surgeon has the duty to delay until he receives the necessary consent for the additional surgery.

Implied consent also applies in emergency situations. If the emergency involves risk to the patient's life, or the patient is unable to give consent due to unconsciousness, coma or other incompetence, it has been held that the patient would have consented to the treatment if he or she were able, thus consent is implied in such situations.

The existence of the emergency should be entered into the medical records, including the reason why the procedure was necessary, e.g., the patient's airway was blocked and an emergency tracheotomy was necessary or the patient would have choked to death.

Patient Abandonment

Once a health care provider undertakes treatment of a patient, this relationship ceases only when the course of treatment has ended, or by mutual consent of the parties. The health care provider must obtain the patient's consent if he or she wishes to withdraw from the relationship earlier.

To avoid liability for abandonment, the health care provider should give the patient written notice of his or her intention to withdraw, the reasons for the withdrawal, and set forth a reasonable period of time for the patient to obtain alternative care.

It is often the case that the health care provider wishes to withdraw from the relationship due to concerns over the patient's failure to follow the medical advice given, thus exposing the health care provider to additional liability if the patient suffers harm as a result. Such reasons for withdrawing from the relationship should be explicitly stated in the written notice of withdrawal given to the patient.

Breach of Contract/Breach of Warranty

Breach of contract and breach of warranty are additional theories of liability which are often advanced, sometimes as a means to extend the applicable statute of limitations. For example, if the health care provider guarantees a particular result from a procedure, e.g. plastic surgery, this guarantee forms the basis of an oral contract. If the patient is not satisfied with the outcome of the procedure, a claim may be made based on a breach of warranty theory.

Breach of Privacy

The medical records of a patient are privileged and confidential information. The release of such information to third parties without the patient's consent is a breach of the patient's privacy and may be actionable. Nevertheless, the law permits discussion of the patient's condition with another health care provider charged with the patient's care, in the context of the treatment.

The topic of medical records is discussed more fully in Chapter 6 of this almanac.

CHAPTER 3:
RESPONSIBLE PARTIES AND THEIR DEFENSES

RESPONSIBLE PARTIES

Medical malpractice is not limited to physicians but may also be committed by a number of health care professionals, including nurses, hospitals, mental health professionals, anesthesiologists, and other persons or entities that provide medical care. When determining which parties to name as defendants in a medical malpractice action, any physician or other health care provider, including hospital employees, should be included. For the purposes of this almanac, the term "health care provider" is used as a general reference to all potentially liable health care professionals.

Vicarious Liability

When third persons are held liable for the conduct of others, they are said to be vicariously liable. We assume both the identity of the actor and the wrongful nature of his conduct, and ask whether liability may be extended beyond the actor to include persons who have not committed a wrong or directly caused any harm, but on whose behalf the wrongdoing actor acted. The concept of vicarious liability is one of considerable practical importance to the plaintiff because it is an effective means of providing a financially responsible defendant. For example, in a hospital liability case, the hospital may be held liable for the torts of their nurse employees. This principle is derived from the common law master/servant relationship and is known as the doctrine of "respondeat superior." This doctrine, as well as other forms of vicarious liability relationships, are explained below.

Respondeat Superior

The most important principle establishing vicarious liability for the tortious conduct of another is the doctrine of respondeat superior: A master is vicariously liable for the torts of his servants committed while the latter are acting within the scope of their employment. The "servant" need not be performing precisely the activity for which he was hired in order to expose the master to liability, and the tortious conduct need not involve physical injury. Thus, the officers of our major corporations are considered "servants" in the legal sense of the word. Also, the "servant" need not be receiving a wage, but may be performing services out of a sense of friendship for another.

Under the doctrine of respondeat superior, a health care provider may be held liable for the acts or omissions of employees or partners. For example, a hospital or nursing home would be held liable for negligent acts committed by the nurses and other caretakers it employs.

In contrast to "servants," independent contractors are persons hired to do jobs under circumstances which, as a general rule, do not call for the application of the doctrine of respondeat superior. If the tortfeasor is an independent contractor, the general rule is that the employer is not vicariously liable for the harm caused by the contractor's wrongful conduct. For example, a hospital is generally not responsible for attending physicians who perform operations at the hospital. unless the hospital had some independent liability—e.g., it negligently granted privileges to an unlicensed doctor.

The topic of Hospital Liability is discussed more fully in Chapter 5 of this almanac.

Liability for Referrals

If a health care provider refers a patient to another health care provider—such as a specialist—who commits malpractice and harms the patient, the primary health care provider would generally not be held liable, unless he knew or should have known that the specialist was likely to perform negligently.

Pharmaceutical Manufacturers

As set forth in Chapter 2, if a patient suffers injuries as a result of a particular medication prescribed by his or her physician, he or she can bring a lawsuit against the drug manufacturer under all of the usual product liability theories—e.g., strict liability, negligence, and breach of warranty, but only if the manufacturer was to blame. If it was the physician's conduct which was at fault—e.g., for not heeding the warnings and information provided by the manufacturer—then the physician may be sued for medical negligence in a medical malpractice lawsuit.

DEFENSES

Once it has been established that there is indeed liability for the injuries sustained by the plaintiff, any available defenses must be determined. The defendant sets forth its defenses in its formal answer to the allegations contained in the plaintiff's complaint. Depending on the jurisdiction, some of those defenses are statutory, therefore, the reader is again cautioned to check the law of their own jurisdictions. Some of the most common defenses to medical malpractice claims are set forth below.

Statute of Limitations

The statute of limitations defense is common to all claims. In general, a statute of limitations refers to any law which sets forth a time period within which a claimant must bring a lawsuit to avoid being barred from enforcing a right or claim.

Most jurisdictions have shortened the statute of limitations as it applies to medical malpractice claims. The case must be filed before the expiration date or risk dismissal. The statute generally begins to run from the date of injury, discovery of the injury, or the date that the injury should reasonably have been discovered.

Tolling the Statute of Limitations

The statute of limitations may be tolled—that is, suspended—under certain circumstances, such as in situations where there has been intentional concealment or fraud on the part of the defendant, or where a foreign object is discovered in the patient's body.

For example, Mr. Smith undergoes an appendectomy in January. Unbeknownst to him, a suturing needle is accidentally left in his abdominal cavity. However, the needle is in a position which is undetectable until several years later when it shifts and causes Mr. Smith excruciating pain. This discovery of a foreign object in Mr. Smith's body would serve as a toll to the statute of limitations.

Further, if during routine x-rays following the surgery, Doctor X became aware that the needle had been left in Mr. Smith, and failed to disclose this fact, this would constitute concealment which also serves to toll the statute.

The tolling provisions in this case are justified because, under the circumstances, it would be unfair to deny Mr. Smith his day in court because the statute may have expired by the time he suffered injury from the negligent act. Further, if Doctor X had not concealed the negligence, the needle could have been removed and Mr. Smith could have been spared the subsequent pain and suffering.

The statute may also be tolled when there exists a statutory disability to bringing the action, such as infancy.

A table of state statutes of limitations in medical malpractice cases is set forth at Appendix 7.

Assumption of Risk/Consent or Release Forms

Assumption of risk refers to the common-law doctrine which states that a plaintiff may not recover for an injury when he has voluntarily exposed himself to a known danger. For example, in a medical malpractice case, the defendant may set forth a defense alleging that the patient assumed the risk by either signing a consent form or a release form. However, such consent or release would not limit the health care provider's liability for negligence, even if the form purports to excuse the health care provider from acts of negligence. Such a provision would likely be unenforceable on public policy grounds.

Absence of Proximate Cause

If the plaintiff cannot prove that the act of malpractice caused the injury, the defendant will prevail. Proximate causation must be rooted in fact—the cause-in-fact—and supported by a legal connection between the action and the injury.

If there was an independent, intervening cause which breaks the causal connection between the first health care provider's negligent act and the intervening act, then the first health care provider may be excused from liability. However, if the intervening act was foreseeable, it would not be sufficient to break the causal connection.

For example, Mr. Smith falls and injures his left wrist. He goes to his physician, Doctor X, who determines, without taking an x-ray, that the injury is a simple sprain. Doctor X prescribes painkillers. A week later, Mr. Smith is still experiencing excruciating pain and, during the night, he decides to visit the hospital emergency room. His wrist is x-rayed and is found to be broken. However, the bones have begun to set abnormally and must be re-broken and re-set.

Mr. Smith is taken to the operating room and sedated. When he wakes up, he discovers that his right wrist is bandaged and he is still experiencing pain in his left wrist. The hospital staff physician misinterpreted the x-ray and performed the procedure on the wrong wrist.

This extraordinary act of malpractice cannot be deemed a foreseeable consequence of Doctor X's negligent misdiagnosis of the broken left wrist. Therefore, Doctor X would not likely be held liable for the injuries sustained to Mr. Smith's right wrist. Nevertheless, Doctor X may still be held liable for his own act of malpractice and its natural consequences.

APPORTIONMENT OF LIABILITY

In cases where there is more than one defendant who is liable, or in which the plaintiff has been determined to be negligent to some degree, it is important to determine the extent of each defendant's liability, as well as its apportionment among the other defendants,

Contributory and Comparative Negligence

Contributory negligence refers to those situations in which the plaintiff's own actions contribute in some way to their harm. Contributory negligence refers to conduct on the part of the plaintiff which falls below the standard to which he should conform for his own protection, and which is a legally contributing cause cooperating with the negligence of the defendant in bringing the plaintiff harm.

For example, the defendant may allege as a defense that the plaintiff's own actions contributed in some way to his or her injury—e.g., the patient failed to take the prescribed medication. The burden of proving the plaintiff's contributory fault is on the defense. Depending on the jurisdiction, the plaintiff's contributory negligence may be a complete bar to recovery.

Comparative negligence refers to a statute change introduced in many jurisdictions to counteract the harshness of the recovery rules of contributory negligence. Under comparative negligence rules, recovery may be diminished, but only according to the plaintiff's degree of culpability.

Depending on the jurisdiction, comparative negligence is also applied to determine the apportionment of liability for each of the defendants where there is more than one defendant, or where there is another party responsible for the injuries sustained by the plaintiff who was not included as a defendant in the lawsuit.

A table of state contributory and comparative negligence rules is set forth at Appendix 8.

Joint and Several Liability

Depending on the jurisdiction, joint and several liability may be imposed when multiple parties are responsible for the plaintiff's injury. Case law has held that when two defendants are both negligent, but only one of them could have caused the plaintiff's injury, the court will hold both of them liable if it cannot determine which of the defendants caused the damage. In such a case, it is the defendants who must come forward with evidence to absolve themselves. This shifts the burden of proof to the defendants. Otherwise, the plaintiff would never be able to prove who actually caused the injury.

An example involves an unexplained injury which occurs during a medical procedure to a part of the body not under treatment. The doctrine of res ipsa loquitur ("the thing speaks for itself") applies against all of the doctors and medical employees who take part in caring for the patient. If the plaintiff were required to prove who was responsible for the injury, it is possible that the medical personnel would keep silent to avoid implicating a colleague and the injured plaintiff would never recover.

A table of state statutes governing joint and several liability is set forth at Appendix 9.

Liability of Joint Enterprise

When two or more persons join together in an enterprise in which each has an equal right to control the other's conduct, one might apply master-servant concepts upon each participant in relation to the other participant. For example, in a medical partnership, each doctor is generally liable for the acts of the other doctors who are partners of the firm.

Liability of Successor Corporation

When Corporation A and Corporation B conduct a formal merger and become Corporation C, C is liable for the torts that A and B may have committed prior to the merger. For example, this may occur in the medical malpractice setting when two hospitals merge.

Death of an Injured Party Prior to Judgment

One may be under the impression that if the injured party dies before there is a recovery, the defendant is "off the hook." However, by statute, the death of the injured party prior to judgment has far less devastating effects upon existing or potential rights to recover against a tortious defendant. Two types of statutes accomplish this result:

Survival Statutes

Survival Statutes prevent abatement of existing causes of action due to the death of either party. The basic measure of recovery is what the decedent would have been able to recover for the injuries if he had survived.

Wrongful Death Statutes

Wrongful death statutes create causes of action that allow recovery when the tortious conduct of the defendant causes someone to die. The basic measure of recovery is the harm caused to the decedent's family by the defendant's conduct.

CHAPTER 4:
DAMAGES

IN GENERAL

Once it has been determined that there is liability, the question turns to whether damages were caused as a result of the wrongful conduct. In medical malpractice cases, as in all personal injury law, damages are usually measured in terms of monetary compensation. There are three categories of money damages recoverable in a personal injury case: (1) compensatory damages; (2) punitive damages, and (3) nominal damages.

COMPENSATORY DAMAGES

Compensatory damages represent an attempt to compensate the injured party for the actual harm he suffered, by awarding the amount of money necessary to restore the plaintiff to his pre-injury condition. Often, a complete restoration cannot be accomplished.

For example, if the malpractice results in loss of a limb, the plaintiff can never be "restored" to their pre-injury condition no matter how much money he or she is awarded.

In such cases, damages also include the monetary value of the difference between the plaintiff's pre-injury and post-injury conditions.

It should be noted that, in medical malpractice cases, the degree of the health care provider's negligence does not translate into the damage award. The damages are directly related to making the plaintiff "whole." The plaintiff is entitled to an award of damages that restores him or her to their pre-injury status, in terms of monetary compensation.

The general rule is "you take your patient as you find him or her." Thus, a health care provider who commits a minor negligent act may end up paying much more than one who commits a severely negligent act, depending on the patient's resulting status.

For example, a patient may have had a pre-existing condition which was aggravated by the negligent act, resulting in severe harm; or one patient may have been highly-paid prior to the injury and, therefore, suffered a huge loss of earnings as a result of the negligent act.

Thus, it is the harm suffered, and not the degree of negligence, which is taken into account in computing the damage award.

Typical items included in compensatory damage awards are listed below.

Medical Expenses

Medical expenses are the most concrete and objectively demonstrable items to identify. The expense must be reasonably related to the defendant's wrongful conduct.

Lost Earnings and Impairment of Earning Capacity

Lost earnings and impairment of earning capacity are the most justifiable element of a general compensatory damages award from a strictly economic point of view. Recovery is sought for:

(1) the earnings actually lost up to the time of the trial or settlement; and

(2) the diminution in the plaintiff's capacity to earn in the future.

Pain, Suffering, and Other Intangible Elements

Pain and suffering is the most difficult element of recovery to measure. This is a broad concept, which may include a number of more or less separate factors, the most common of which is the physical pain associated with the injury. Recovery for mental suffering associated with bodily disfigurement may also be included as an element of pain and suffering.

Another element is the loss of enjoyment in relation to life in either all of its aspects, or merely certain aspects. This is also known as hedonic damages.

For example, if a plaintiff enjoyed playing piano as a hobby, and has suffered an injury to his hands, the plaintiff has suffered a loss of enjoyment in relation to the ability to play the piano.

Of course, if the particular activity involved the plaintiff's livelihood, the damages for loss of earning capacity would also be included, and would greatly increase the measure of damages.

PUNITIVE DAMAGES

Punitive damages involve an award of a substantial amount of money to the plaintiff for the purpose of punishing the defendant. Thus, punitive damages are usually only awarded if the health care provider engaged in reckless or grossly negligent conduct, or acted intentionally.

Liability insurance is the usual source of recovery for medical malpractice claims. However, in cases involving intentional torts, such as battery, insurance generally does not cover the wrongdoer. In the absence of insurance coverage, claims must be paid out of the defendant's personal assets.

NOMINAL DAMAGES

A nominal damages award involves a very small amount of money, awarded merely for the purpose of showing that the plaintiff was legally wronged, particularly where the injuries sustained, if any, are inconsequential.

STATUTORY LIMITS ON DAMAGE AWARDS

The calculation of economic damages is generally quite predictable in that it requires a computation of the plaintiff's past and future economic costs as a result of the injury. Most of these expenses are easily obtainable, concrete figures. The most difficult to compute would be items such as future lost earnings, due to unpredictability of inflation and salary increases.

However, it is the non-economic damages, such as pain and suffering, and loss of enjoyment of life, which are the most difficult to assess, and which sometimes result in significant jury awards. Further, in appropriate cases, punitive damage awards—also unrelated to the actual injury—may be sizeable. It is this unpredictability which concerns the insurance carriers.

Many of these non-economic damage awards are very disproportionate to the economic damage awards, particularly when the plaintiff's injury is grievous, or where the health care provider's conduct was outrageous, because in such cases, the jury likes to send a strong message.

Because these high costs of litigation are eventually passed on to public, e.g. by raising insurance premiums and limiting the range of covered health care services, many states have enacted legislation to place a cap on the jury awards.

A table of state statutes governing limits on damage awards in medical malpractice cases is set forth at Appendix 10.

Some states offer state-sponsored liability insurance for physicians and/or operate patient compensation funds. A patient compensation fund functions as a system of excess insurance for health care providers. Although state requirements vary, in general, to become a "qualified provider," entitled to the benefits, a health care provider must generally file proof of financial responsibility and pay a state-assessed surcharge, which is used to support the fund.

A qualified provider establishes financial responsibility by purchasing malpractice liability insurance in the statutorily prescribed amount. The maximum liability of a qualified provider for an occurrence is limited to the amount of required insurance. The Patient Compensation Fund is liable for the excess over what is owed by all the qualified providers up to the statutory damage cap.

A table of state rules governing patient compensation funds and/or state-sponsored liability insurance for health care providers is set forth at Appendix 11.

COLLATERAL SOURCE RULES

Under the traditional collateral source rules, the injured plaintiff generally recovers most of his or her damages resulting from economic loss from the defendant, even though the plaintiff may have received reimbursement for such expenses from their own private insurance or governmental sources.

However, many states have enacted legislation requiring a plaintiff's damage award to be offset by reimbursement from collateral sources. Some statutes permit the plaintiff a credit for payments made to obtain such coverage, e.g. insurance premium payments.

A table of state collateral source rules in medical malpractice cases is set forth at Appendix 12.

CHAPTER 5:
HOSPITAL LIABILITY

IN GENERAL

Hospitals are corporations which are generally organized as either public or private entities. A public hospital is created by the act of a governmental authority and controlled under the auspices of that government unit by the governing body of the hospital. A private hospital is either (i) voluntary—i.e., a charitable not-for-profit corporation; (ii) investor-owned—operating for profit on behalf of shareholders; or (iii) a member of a multi-unit system which consists of multiple facilities sharing management and services under a single ownership.

As more fully set forth in Chapter 1, The Joint Commission on Accreditation of Healthcare Organizations (JCAHO) is a private accrediting body which promulgates minimal standards of hospital operation and periodically reviews hospital performance.

THE MEDICAL STAFF

The medical staff of a hospital must consist of fully-licensed physicians, and may also include other non-physician licensed individuals, such as dentists, podiatrists and nurse practitioners. The medical staff is responsible for overseeing patient care as well as the professional conduct of its members.

In order to be appointed to the medical staff, an applicant must meet certain minimum professional criteria relating to their education, experience, competence, licensure and health. For example, involvement in medical negligence litigation, loss of license or loss of privileges at another facility will be carefully scrutinized.

A hospital which fails to make reasonable inquiries into the background of an applicant may ultimately be found responsible under the corporate negligence doctrine for negligent supervision or retention if it employs or grants privileges to an incompetent physician.

Grounds for denial of an application for professional privileges may include: (i) The type of education and degree obtained by the applicant. For example, chiropractors are generally excluded; (ii) inadequate professional liability insurance; (iii) behavior and personal conduct; and (iv) the needs of the hospital and its patients.

THE NURSING STAFF

Hospitals are required to establish a nursing department. The nursing department is responsible for establishing standards of nursing care; approving the employment qualifications for its nurses; and conducting evaluations of the staff. The nursing department is also required to set forth an organizational plan delineating lines of responsibility and accountability.

It is the responsibility of a hospital to make sure that a sufficient number of registered nurses are on duty at all times to maintain quality patient care. Hospitals may be held liable for damages resulting from a nursing staff shortage. In considering whether there are a sufficient number of nurses on duty, certain factors will be evaluated, including the number of patients in the unit and the level of care they require; the degree of on-duty staff expertise; the availability of support personnel; and the geographic makeup of the unit.

THEORIES OF LIABILITY

As discussed in Chapter 2, liability for medical malpractice cannot exist unless there is a health care provider/patient relationship which creates a duty on the part of the health care provider to render acceptable medical care to the patient. In the case of a hospital, this would occur when the patient visits the hospital and receives treatment by a hospital employee. Hospitals are now routinely named as defendants in medical malpractice actions under a variety of theories of liability.

The Duty to Treat

Under the common law, an individual was not generally obligated to prevent an injury to another absent special circumstances. This common law doctrine includes the right of a hospital to refuse to admit or treat a person who comes in seeking admission or treatment.

The Courts have generally deferred to the medical judgment of hospital personnel, and refused to require hospitals to use their medical resources for every person seeking treatment. Nevertheless, as further discussed below, there are circumstances under which the Courts have held that the common law doctrine of no duty to admit or treat does not apply.

Emergency Situations

Hospitals are generally required to treat seriously injured or sick persons on an emergency basis, and their refusal to treat such people has resulted in the imposition of liability. However, the nature of an emergency is subjective and it is not always apparent whether a patient's condition actually constitutes an emergency.

In general, emergencies involve events which are sudden or unforeseen. However, even where an individual's condition is not in an emergency status at the time they arrive at the hospital, requiring that person to seek medical attention elsewhere may turn a non-emergency situation into an emergency. Thus, a hospital may also be required to prevent the occurrence of an emergency.

If a medical screening examination determines that the individual has an emergency medical condition, they may not be transferred or discharged unless their medical condition is stabilized. An exception to the rule exists if the patient requests a transfer, in writing, after being thoroughly advised of the risks of the transfer and the hospital's obligation to treat the patient. In addition, another exception exists if a physician certifies that the medical benefits of the transfer outweigh the risks.

Discrimination

Many federal and state statutes prohibit unreasonable discrimination by hospitals in their refusal to admit or treat, despite the common law doctrine. For example, hospitals are constitutionally prohibited from refusing to treat or admit a particular person due to their race, color, religion or national origin. In addition, hospitals are not permitted to discriminate against patients based on their inability to pay for their treatment, particularly where the hospital receives federal assistance.

The Doctrine of Respondeat Superior

Hospitals have historically enjoyed limited liability under malpractice law insofar as they were not liable for the acts of the physicians who used their facilities to treat patients. However, as set forth in Chapter 3, under the doctrine of "respondeat superior," hospitals have been deemed vicariously liable for the negligence of their own employees.

For a hospital to be vicariously liable for an employee, the employee must have been acting within the scope of his or her employment. The hospital would not generally be liable for intentional acts of an employee, unless the particular act was foreseeable. The doctrine of respondeat superior has been held to apply to a hospital's residents, interns, nurses and other hospital health care providers and employees. Courts have also held that physician "employees" are servants for this purpose as well.

Attending Physicians

Historically, hospitals have enjoyed limited liability and exposure in connection with the medical negligence of attending physicians who use their facilities to treat their private patients. This was based on the nature of the relationship between the hospital and the physician, and the view that the hospital was merely a "hotel" which provided facilities for the patients of the physicians to whom it grants privileges to practice.

A hospital will generally assert that the respondeat superior doctrine does not apply to an attending physician because he or she is an independent contractor and not an employee. Nevertheless, as discussed below, a hospital may still be found liable for its own independent negligence in selecting and granting privileges to an incompetent physician.

Corporate Negligence Doctrine

The corporate negligence doctrine has developed in response to the limited liability enjoyed by a hospital concerning the negligent care rendered by an attending physician who uses hospital facilities. The corporate negligence doctrine seeks to hold hospitals, as corporations, liable for their own independent negligence based on the breach of a duty owed "directly" to the patient.

Under the corporate negligence doctrine, a hospital is obligated to use reasonable care in granting privileges to an attending physician. Thus, if a hospital failed to properly investigate the credentials of an attending physician before granting them privileges, or if a hospital knew or should have known that the physician was incompetent based on its information, the hospital may be liable for negligently granting privileges.

Other Bases for Independent Hospital Liability

A hospital may also be independently liable if its own employees fail to follow a private attending physician's orders. For example, hospital employees, such as nurses, are not permitted to supersede the course of treatment established by the private attending physician. However, hospital liability may also arise if the private attending physician's course of treatment is clearly contraindicated, and hospital employees do not make a reasonable inquiry of the physician as to his treatment plan.

The hospital also has a duty of care owed directly to its patients which is independent of any duty owed the patient by the attending physician. For example, hospital employees are obligated to observe and record the condition of its patients so that the attending physician may render the appropriate treatment.

Other independent duties which Courts have determined give rise to hospital liability include the duty to protect the patient from harm; the duty to adequately perform clinical tests; the duty to keep accurate medical records; and the duty to properly admit and discharge a patient.

DISCHARGE AGAINST MEDICAL ADVICE

If a patient seeks discharge from the hospital against the medical advice of the treating physician, it is important that the patient be thoroughly advised of the risks associated with premature discharge. This is generally known as "informed refusal" to treatment, and should be carefully documented in the patient's medical chart should the patient suffer injuries as a result of their decision. In addition, the patient should be required to sign a release form absolving hospital personnel from any injuries caused by the release against medical advice.

For a more detailed discussion of hospital negligence, the reader is advised to consult this author's legal almanac entitled Hospital Liability Law, also published by Oceana Publishing Company.

NURSING HOME MALPRACTICE

Many nursing homes are merely residential facilities which provide room and board, and daily activities for the residents. There are generally no medical services available. Thus, if a resident sustains injuries in such a nursing home, or suffers physical neglect, a cause of action would likely be for general negligence as opposed to medical malpractice.

A skilled nursing facility does provide medical care to its residents, who are likely in need of such special medical services. A skilled nursing home employs health care providers, such as nurses, and may be liable for medical malpractice should a health care provider render negligent medical care to a resident.

The most likely medical malpractice claim to arise in a nursing home would include medical neglect, e.g., a lack of care for existing medical problems of a resident. This could include, for example, failure to prevent dehydration and malnutrition; negligence in providing medication and failure to provide reasonable access to medical services, etc.

In order to reduce the possibility of medical negligence in the nursing home setting, family members should investigate the background of the medical staff, e.g., registered nurses, licensed practical nurses, and nursing assistants. Find out the credentials and what type of training these nurses have and whether they are trained in the area of your family member's diagnosis. For example, if your family member is suffering from Alzheimer's Disease, determine whether the medical staff at the nursing home has experience working with such patients. In addition, find out the ratio of nurses to residents, and the level of need required by the other residents, to ensure that there is adequate medical coverage.

There are services that provide information on nursing homes for a fee. One such service is Senior Care Resources, Inc., which provides the public with comprehensive and detailed reports on nursing homes.

CHAPTER 6:
MEDICAL RECORDS

CONFIDENTIALITY

A patient's medical records are considered highly confidential due to the personal nature of the information contained in the records. For this reason, the patient is required to give a written authorization releasing those records to any third parties. In the context of a medical malpractice case, the plaintiff's attorney as well as the defendant's attorney will request that the plaintiff sign authorizations for the release of medical records. In the case of a minor child, the parent or legal guardian of the child can authorize the release of the child's medical records. Of course, the patient has an absolute right to obtain a copy of his or her medical records.

There are also laws which provide extra confidentiality protection for certain types of medical records. The purpose for the extra protection is to encourage people who may suffer from certain medical conditions, for which the patient may be particularly sensitive or embarrassed, to seek medical treatment. For example, federal law protects substance abuse treatment records. In addition, some states require special authorization for release of mental health records and/or records relating to HIV/AIDS.

CONTENTS OF THE MEDICAL RECORD

A medical record may be very difficult to decipher for a layperson with no medical background. The handwriting is often illegible, and many notations are abbreviated. In addition, much of the medical terminology used in medical records is derived from Latin. Therefore, a working knowledge of medical terminology is helpful when reviewing medical records.

Charts containing commonly used medical terms, and the meanings of prefixes, roots and suffixes in medical terminology, are set forth at Appendices 13, 14, 15, and 16, respectively.

A complete hospital record generally includes the following materials:

Certification

Upon request, an authorized employee of the hospital's Medical Records Department will provide a signed document certifying that the copy of the hospital record has been compared with the original and is a true and complete copy. The certification may be used in support of having the medical record introduced as evidence in court.

Physician Attestation Statement

The physician attestation statement—also known as the identification sheet—is usually the first page of the hospital record. This document generally contains admission and discharge information, and is signed by a physician.

The admission information usually consists of the patient's background and insurance information, and the admitting diagnosis. Upon discharge, this document also sets forth the final diagnosis, any complications and secondary diagnoses, and any procedures performed, including surgical procedures.

Admission Record

The admission record contains information about the patient's medical history and the findings of his or her physical examination upon admission, including the results of laboratory and other testing, such as x-rays and MRIs. This document also contains the history of the patient's present illness or injury, and the course of treatment to be followed.

Consent Forms

The hospital record includes any consent forms signed by the patient, including consent to treatment, surgery and anesthesia, and other procedures. The forms are generally filled out upon admission and at other times during the patient's hospitalization when a particular procedure may be required.

Progress Notes

The progress notes include the attending physician's chronological record of developments that occur during a patient's hospitalization. These notations are generally made during routine hospital rounds and upon any significant change in the patient's condition or treatment.

Nursing Notes and Flow Charts

Depending on the hospital, a nurse's progress notes may be contained within the physician's progress notes, or may be contained in a separate section known as a flow chart. Nurse's notes generally include information and observations about the patient gathered during each shift, including the patient's physical, mental and emotional state; medications administered; vital signs such as blood pressure and pulse; food intake; personal hygiene and bathroom habits; any signification changes in the patient's condition; and discharge instructions and notes.

Doctor's Orders

The Doctor's Orders section of the hospital records contains the physician's instructions to the nursing staff concerning the patient's treatment and care, including medications and dosages; dietary requirements; and laboratory tests, etc.

Laboratory Reports

The laboratory reports may include blood and urine analyses; x-ray reports; MRI reports; electrocardiographs and the results of other diagnostic studies.

Requests for Consultation

The consultation request reports generally involve a request from the attending physician to another consulting physician for an opinion or some other assistance relating to the patient's treatment. The consulting physician will either enter his or her own report or add a notation to the attending physician's progress notes.

Discharge Summary

The discharge summary is the attending physician's overview of the patient's hospitalization and includes a restatement of the admitting history and physical examination, the patient's hospital course, diagnoses, results of diagnostic studies, treatment given, and disposition. The summary is generally dictated and transcribed on the day of discharge.

UNAUTHORIZED DISCLOSURE OF MEDICAL RECORDS

Information concerning an individual's medical condition is of interest to a number of entities for a variety of reasons, including insurance carriers, employers, health care providers, government agencies, and law enforcement. Technological advances have made accessing, disseminating and sharing an individual's medical records relatively easy and swift. However, without legal safeguards, there is the potential for virtually unlimited access to an individual's medical records without his or her knowledge or consent.

The danger in allowing the unauthorized dissemination of an individual's medical records is that certain entities may adversely use this information to the patient's detriment. For example, insurance carriers may refuse to issue life and health insurance policies to those individuals they deem as risks based on their medical history.

In addition, employers may be unwilling to employ individuals who they deem are unhealthy based on their medical records. In fact, a study by the University of Illinois found that thirty five percent (35%) of Fortune 500 companies admitted to checking medical records prior to hiring or promoting employees.

Further, law enforcement agencies may access and use an individual's medical records obtained without authorization or warrant as evidence in connection with the prosecution of a criminal matter, e.g. for identification purposes.

Unfortunately, there is presently no comprehensive national policy ensuring the privacy of an individual's medical records, although some states have enacted laws in an attempt to protect their citizens from a breach of their privacy.

THE MEDICAL INFORMATION PRIVACY AND SECURITY ACT OF 1999 (S. 573)

In an attempt to protect the medical privacy of individual citizens, Congress has introduced legislation—The Medical Information Privacy and Security Act of 1999—which would require an individual's informed consent before his or her records were disclosed to third parties, except under carefully delineated circumstances.

For example, the law would permit personally identifiable medical records to be disclosed to a public health authority without consent only where the information relates to a specific public health purpose.

In addition, recognizing the societal value of medical research, the law does not restrict the use of anonymous or de-identified medical records for such research, but does regulate medical research that uses medical records containing personally identifiable information.

Further, disclosure of protected health information in civil litigation could occur only after it has been established that the information is material to the adjudication, e.g., where a litigant has placed his or her medical condition at issue.

Finally, the proposed legislation would greatly limit law enforcement access to medical records. For example, the proposed legislation requires law enforcement officers to obtain a court order, warrant or grand jury subpoena before gaining access to medical records. In addition, the law enforcement agent who wants to view medical records would be required to demonstrate probable cause to believe that:

1. The information is relevant and material to an ongoing criminal investigation;

2. The investigative needs of the agent cannot reasonably be satisfied by de-identified health information or by any other information; and

3. The law enforcement need for the information outweighs the privacy interest of the individual to whom the information pertains.

In effect, the legislation would provide a Fourth Amendment-like standard to the acquisition of an individual's medical records maintained by third parties.

In addition, the legislation further limits the use of protected health information following disclosure. For example, where protected health information has been disclosed in one investigation, it cannot be used in any other investigation unless the subsequent investigation arises out of, or is directly related to, the investigation for which the protected health information was initially obtained.

Further, the proposed legislation requires that notice be given to the individual whose records are being sought. The individual is also given the opportunity to contest to the release of this information.

Selected text from the Medical Information Privacy and Security Act of 1999 (S. 573) is set forth at Appendix 17.

PRE-LITIGATION MEDICAL RECORDS REVIEW

An individual who believes they have been the victim of medical negligence can have their medical records evaluated by health care professionals to determine whether there was a deviation from the applicable standard of care. There are companies who will perform this service for the patient even before the patient has retained an attorney to handle the case. Along with their medical records, the patient submits a statement of the facts and any questions he or she may want answered concerning their medical treatment. For an agreed upon fee, the patient receives a comprehensive written review of their case and whether it forms the basis for a medical malpractice claim.

A sample agreement for the review of medical records is set forth at Appendix 18.

If it is determined that the patient has a viable medical malpractice claim, he or she can provide the report to their attorney, who will be able to proceed with a formal action. The report will serve as proof of merit of the case in those jurisdictions which require the attorney to file a Certificate of Merit in order to initiate legal action. Obtaining such a report increases the likelihood that an attorney will take a case that he or she would otherwise be reluctant to accept due to the questionable nature of the medical issues involved.

CHAPTER 7:
MEDICAL MALPRACTICE LITIGATION

RETAINING AN ATTORNEY

A medical malpractice action begins with the injured patient making contact with an attorney, at which point an initial meeting will be arranged. The attorney's first meeting with the client generally includes a detailed discussion of the facts which support the client's medical malpractice claim. The attorney may also request to see the medical records for a preliminary review.

If the attorney is satisfied that the case has merit and agrees to accept the case, the client will be required to sign a retainer agreement. The retainer agreement generally sets forth the terms of compensation, costs and services to be provided. In states where legal fees are limited by statute, the legal fees set forth in the retainer agreement should reflect those limits.

A sample retainer agreement in a medical malpractice case is set forth at Appendix 19.

Medical malpractice cases are generally taken on a contingency fee basis. This means that the attorney does not receive a legal fee unless there is a recovery. The client is also responsible for the payment of disbursements—e.g., court filing fees, expert witness fees, etc.—despite the outcome of the case. However, most attorneys will advance those costs and seek reimbursement from the recovery. Many states have set limits on the legal fees an attorney can charge in a medical malpractice action. Generally, the contingency percentage decreases as the award increases.

A table of state statutes governing attorney fees in medical malpractice cases is set forth at Appendix 20.

INVESTIGATING THE CLAIM

Special Statutory Requirements in Medical Malpractice Actions

It has been argued that an unprecedented increase in medical malpractice claims and large jury verdicts have brought about a medical malpractice litigation crisis, causing the insurance rates of health care providers to soar. There is concern that this will in turn cause health care costs to rise and drive health care providers from the profession because of their inability to maintain liability coverage.

To try and address these concerns, a number of states have enacted special statutory requirements that must be satisfied before a medical malpractice action is initiated. For example, some states require the parties to submit to arbitration, a process which is more fully discussed below. Other states have created special malpractice panels to screen claims.

Some states have certain procedural rules which must be followed which are unique to medical malpractice actions, such as a showing of merit in order to file a medical malpractice action. This generally means that a physician must review the records and indicate to the attorney that there appears to be some departure from accepted medical practices. Depending on the state, the attorney may be required to file a Certificate of Merit which confirms that the attorney has consulted with a physician and, based upon that consultation, the action has merit.

A sample Certificate of Merit is set forth at Appendix 21.

Further, as set forth in Chapter 4, in an effort to reign in what some perceive as excessive jury verdicts, many states have enacted limits on the damages the plaintiff may recover.

Thus, the reader is advised to check the law of their jurisdiction to determine whether there are any special statutory requirements before filing a medical malpractice action.

Gathering Medical Evidence

In preparing a medical negligence case against a hospital, physician, or other health care provider, one must first obtain all relevant medical records for review. The patient has an absolute right to a copy of his or her medical record. In order to obtain a copy of the medical record, an authorization for the release of the records must be signed by the patient or, in the case of a minor, by his or her parent or legal guardian. The release is then sent to the medical records department of the hospital or other health care provider.

A sample Medical Records Release is set forth at Appendix 22.

The hospital or health care provider will generally charge a fee for copying the records. Some hospitals hire outside companies to undertake the task of copying the records and billing the patient. Many jurisdictions place a statutory cap on the amount a health care provider may charge for copying the records. For example, in New York, the Public Health Law limits the fee to 75 cents per page. The reader is advised to check the law of his or her jurisdiction concerning the applicable fee.

Prior to filing the lawsuit, the attorney will make a careful evaluation of all medical records, including the hospital record. The records should not be limited to the malpractice, but should include any other relevant medical care that the client underwent, even if it appears not to relate to the malpractice. For example, a review of prior records may be necessary to determine whether a pre-existing condition or treatment has any connection to the present injury.

A thorough review of all medical records is essential. A necessary element in all medical negligence cases is a deviation from the standard of care, and the medical record is a primary source of such evidence. The attorney may engage a health care professional to assist in deciphering the medical language. However, a working knowledge of medical terminology is advantageous to the attorney.

Lists of commonly used medical terms, and the meanings of roots, prefixes and suffixes used in medical terms, are set forth at Appendices 13, 14, 15, and 16.

Further, all of the patient's documentation concerning the malpractice, including any personal journal or notes they may have kept concerning the events must be scrutinized. In addition, copies of prescriptions and billing records should be reviewed. One never knows where a crucial bit of information may be located.

Background and Credentials of Defendant

A thorough investigation into the background of the defendant health care provider or medical facility should also be undertaken. Sources of information include state licensing agencies, medical boards, and medical and/or other professional schools the defendant may have attended. The investigator should also conduct a routine investigation of the defendant's criminal records, motor vehicle records, and property and asset records. An investigation of court files to see whether the defendant has ever been sued before may provide important information.

It is important to check the credentials of all of the potential defendants in a medical malpractice action. Where a physician holds himself out as a specialist in a particular area, it is important to find out whether that physician is "board-certified." A board-certified physician has satisfied certain post-graduate requirements, such as additional training in the specialty area, and has passed an examination given by the board governing that specialty. If a physician who holds himself out as a specialist is not board-certified in the particular field, an inference may be made that he or she does not, in fact, possess the additional training and skills that should be achieved, and such lack of training and skill may have been the cause of the alleged malpractice.

Chapter 1 sets forth many of the resources available to the public in investigating the background and credentials of a health care provider or medical facility.

THE LITIGATION PROCESS

Medical malpractice litigation is formal, time-consuming, complicated, costly, and can go on for years. The parties to the litigation are each responsible for developing their own legal theory, and providing their evidence, in order to prove their case and prevail in the dispute. The judge or jury considers all of the evidence and arguments set forth by the parties. Once the parties have set forth their case, the judge or jury is entrusted to make the final decision.

The Summons and Complaint

The medical malpractice lawsuit is officially begun when service of a summons and complaint is made upon the defendant. Service is undertaken by a person authorized by law to serve legal documents, such as the sheriff or a process server. Many jurisdictions also permit a non-party, over the age of 18, to serve legal documents.

The complaint details the plaintiff's malpractice claim against the defendant, and sets forth the legal theory under which the plaintiff seeks to prevail. The plaintiff may set forth more than one legal theory. For example, common medical malpractice allegations may include negligence, lack of informed consent, and breach of contract. The plaintiff must be able to prove the essential elements of the theory set forth in order to prevail.

A sample medical malpractice complaint for wrongful death and negligence against a hospital is set forth at Appendix 23.

The lawsuit must be filed within the statutorily prescribed period of time for medical malpractice actions. This time period is referred to as the statute of limitations. Most states have enacted shortened statutes of limitations for medical malpractice actions.

A table setting forth the state statutes of limitations for medical malpractice cases is set forth at Appendix 7.

The Answer

Upon receipt of the summons and complaint, the defendant must respond to the complaint within a prescribed period of time or risk losing the dispute by default. The defendant may serve an answer to the complaint, or may choose to make a motion seeking to dismiss the complaint prior to serving his or her answer.

These preliminary motions are usually based on some technical point, such as improper service or lack of jurisdiction. If the motion is granted, the case is dismissed. However, if the motion is denied, the defendant must serve an answer within a statutorily defined time period following the decision on the motion.

The defendant's answer admits or denies the allegations set forth in the complaint, and presents any defenses to the allegations that the defendant may have. At this point, the defendant may choose to include counterclaims—such as nonpayment of medical services—which must in turn be "answered" by the plaintiff in a formal response.

Motion Practice

The litigation procedure, from initiation of the lawsuit to final disposition, is governed by the statutory law of the particular court in which the lawsuit is filed. During the pendency of the lawsuit, much of litigation is accomplished on paper. There are numerous motions which a party may file and ask the assigned judge to rule upon. A motion, which may be made orally or in writing, is an application to the court requesting an order or a ruling in favor of the applicant.

For example, a party may make a motion seeking some type of interim relief, such as the production of certain evidence. The notice of motion and any supporting papers are served upon the other party, who usually responds in opposition to the motion.

Discovery

Medical malpractice litigation generally involves a lengthy discovery process. Typical discovery may include the exchange of detailed information, the examination of documents and other evidence, and an oral examination of the parties and prospective witnesses in a proceeding known as a deposition or examination before trial, depending on the jurisdiction.

During a deposition, the deponent is placed under oath, and must answer a series of questions put forth by the attorneys for the parties. The sworn testimony given at the deposition is recorded by a legal stenographer, who prepares a transcript of the deposition for use at trial. The deposition testimony pins down each deponent's version of the facts, and can be used to impeach a party or non-party witness.

Going to Trial

As the lawsuit nears trial, the judge will usually set the matter down for a settlement conference in an attempt to resolve the dispute without going to trial. Absent a successful outcome, the lawsuit will be set down for trial. A jury will be selected by the attorneys and the plaintiff will present his or her case. The defendant will set forth their defenses and, following closing arguments, a decision is rendered by the jury. If it is not a jury trial, the judge will preside over the trial and will render the decision. The parties may seek to appeal unfavorable decisions to higher courts. Once the appeals process has been exhausted, the decision is final and enforceable.

EXPERT TESTIMONY

Most medical malpractice actions require the testimony of an expert witness who has experience in the area of medicine which forms the basis of the lawsuit. The plaintiff's medical expert is called upon to testify for several purposes in the medical malpractice action:

1. To establish the applicable standard of care and demonstrate how it was violated;

2. To establish a causal connection between the negligence and the injury; and

3. To establish the extent of the injury.

The expert witness must be found competent to render his or her opinion in the matter. Thus, the expert must demonstrate that he or she is familiar with the defendant health care provider's specialty area; the medical procedures involved; and the applicable standard of care.

The expert's familiarity generally results from his or her own professional experience in the field. Where the geographic locality of the standard of care is in issue, the expert must be familiar with that setting as well. Once it is found that the expert is competent to testify, the extent of his or her experience would go to the weight given the testimony.

Preparing the Medical Expert

Under the law, the medical expert must base his or her opinion upon a "reasonable medical probability." This basically means that the doctor believes that his or her opinion is more likely than not correct. For example, if the issue is whether a certain medication prescribed for the plaintiff caused the plaintiff's injury, the doctor need only believe that it is more likely than not that the medication caused the plaintiff's injury. It is important to note that the language requires a "probability" not a "possibility." Another often-used phrase is that the medical expert's opinion is based upon a "reasonable medical certainty." Nevertheless, the law does recognize that a degree of uncertainty necessarily exists in most cases.

Under cross-examination, the medical expert may be asked questions which require either a yes or no answer in order to advance the defendant's position. However, answering in this manner often does not take into account other factors necessary to adequately respond. If the medical expert believes that a question cannot be adequately answered with a yes or no answer, he or she generally has the right to explain their answer.

The defense will often use a book or article to try and contradict the medical expert's opinion. However, before a particular book or article can be used to contradict the testimony, the medical expert must agree that the particular book or article is recognized as authoritative in its field. If the expert does not agree that the particular book or article is authoritative, the defense cannot use the material to contradict the expert's prior testimony. Thus, if the medical expert does not believe that a certain article or book presented by the defense is authoritative on the subject matter, they should state that fact.

Expert Compensation

In most cases, the expert will expect to be compensated in return for his or her testimony and expenses. Prior to trial, counsel should have a clear understanding with the expert as to compensation, and who is responsible for payment. The amount of compensation varies with the community and with the medical specialty. Thus, the fee charged by a specialist, such as a heart surgeon, will likely exceed the fee charged by a general practitioner, such as an internist. The expert will either charge for a half-day or whole-day, depending on the amount of time he or she needs to be away from their practice.

The medical expert will likely be questioned by the defense about his or her fee in an effort to discredit their testimony as a "hired gun." The medical expert should honestly and forthrightly respond that they are being compensated for their testimony based upon the amount of time and effort they have expended on the case.

Exceptions to Expert Testimony Requirement

In certain limited situations, expert testimony is not required. This is obviously advantageous for the plaintiff, who often finds it a difficult and costly task to obtain a physician who will testify against another member of the profession.

Defendant Physician Testimony

When the defendant physician has made statements of admission, such as that he or she made a mistake, these statements may be sufficient exceptions to the expert testimony requirement.

The Common Knowledge Exception

The exceptions to the expert testimony requirement include cases in which the negligence is comprehensible to the layperson, such as when the doctrine of "res ipsa loquitur" is invoked. Res ipsa loquitur translates into "the thing speaks for itself." Negligence may be inferred where there has been an unexplained injury of a type that does not normally occur in the absence of negligence.

For example, it does not take an expert opinion to demonstrate to the jury that a surgical tool left inside a patient following surgery infers that negligence must have taken place. Further, to succeed with a res ipsa loquitur claim, the event must have been caused by an agency or instrumentality of the defendant; and must not have been due to any voluntary action or contribution by the plaintiff.

The common knowledge exception has been extended to include cases in which the fact patterns are more complex but still comprehensible to the lay person.

FINAL RESOLUTION OF THE MEDICAL MALPRACTICE CLAIM

The medical malpractice claim is usually resolved upon payment of a sum of money to the plaintiff (a) after trial by verdict of a judge or jury; (b) by arbitration award; or (c) by settlement.

By Verdict

The final stage of the medical malpractice trial occurs when the finder of fact—the judge or jury—renders a verdict for either the plaintiff or the defense. In a bifurcated trial, the issue of liability is resolved first and, if liability is determined, a second trial is held to determine the extent of the damages suffered by the plaintiff, and the apportionment of the liability among the responsible parties.

If there is a defense verdict, the case is dismissed and the plaintiff loses. Of course, the plaintiff always has the option of appealing the decision if there are adequate grounds to support an appeal.

By Arbitration Award

The parties to a medical malpractice claim may choose to resolve the dispute through the process of arbitration, in which case the arbitrator issues a binding decision and sets forth an award of damages. A number of states have enacted legislation which requires and/or permits the parties to submit a medical malpractice case to arbitration. Although voluntary arbitration is most commonly used to decide contract disputes, the arbitration process is being looked upon as a valuable means to resolve medical malpractice disputes in an effort to reduce costs, avoid trial and streamline the litigation process.

Arbitration is the process whereby an impartial third party, known as an arbitrator, listens to both sides of the dispute and issues a binding decision. Arbitration is similar to—but less formal than—a trial before a judge.

Arbitration offers many advantages over litigation. Arbitration is less costly, and disputes are generally resolved in much less time than when they are submitted to the court. Court calendars are backlogged and litigants may wait months or years to have their day in court. In the meantime, the escalating expense of litigation is in many cases prohibitive.

The cost of arbitration is comparatively low, and is more predictable, than litigation. Generally, the parties pay a filing fee, an administration fee, and the arbitrator's fee. However, if the arbitration hearing should be prolonged, the arbitrator's fee can become substantial—and the loser may have to pay all of the expenses of the arbitration hearing.

Nevertheless, there are other disadvantages which may deter some parties from submitting their dispute to arbitration. For example, discovery rights are limited. This means that if a party wishes to hide important information, they will likely succeed. In addition, the parties generally do not have the right to appeal the arbitrator's decision as they would be entitled to do following a judicial decision.

For a more detailed discussion of alternative dispute resolution, the reader is advised to consult this author's legal almanac entitled The Law of Alternative Dispute Resolution, also published by Oceana Publishing Company.

By Settlement

The majority of medical malpractice claims are settled prior to trial. A settlement is a mutual agreement to terminate the dispute for consideration—usually the payment of a sum of money. A settlement may be judicial or non-judicial. A non-judicial settlement is one which is reached between the parties without court intervention. A judicial settlement is one which is reached during the pendency of a lawsuit, usually with the supervision and guidance of the trial judge. In general, the policy of all courts is to encourage settlement and discourage litigation.

Once an agreement has been reached, a final written document encompassing all of the negotiated points should be drafted and signed by the parties. The settlement agreement may also include a release of claims. By signing a release, a party gives up all right to pursue the claims stated in the release. This is both the motivation and consideration for entering into the settlement agreement.

THE ROLE OF THE INSURANCE CARRIER

Liability insurance is the usual source of recovery for medical malpractice claims. However, in cases involving intentional torts, insurance generally does not cover the wrongdoer. In the absence of insurance coverage, claims must be paid out of the defendant's personal assets.

The insurance company has an obligation to settle a case in good faith. If the company is presented with a settlement opportunity that is within the policy limit, it should settle the case unless there is strong evidence that the case has no merit. If the insurance company refuses to settle a meritorious claim, it could be held liable for payment of any excess above the policy limit which may be awarded after trial.

DISBURSEMENT OF FUNDS

Lump Sum Settlement

The lump sum settlement is the most common type of settlement, which generally requires the payment of a sum of money in exchange for the release of the other party's claims. If payment is to be made in a lump sum, once the necessary paperwork has been completed—i.e., the order, arbitration award or settlement agreement—a check or draft is drawn up by the defendant, or its insurance company, and is generally made payable to both the plaintiff client and his or her attorney.

The attorney usually deposits the check in an attorney trust account for disbursement of funds. The costs of litigation are generally deducted from the gross recovery. The attorney then calculates his or her legal fee according to the terms of the retainer agreement, which should correspond to the jurisdiction's statutory provisions governing attorney fees in medical malpractice cases.

Sliding-Scale Settlement

A sliding scale settlement includes a condition in which it is agreed that an adjustment may be made to the settling defendant's obligation dependent upon any amounts which may ultimately be recovered from the nonsettling defendants.

Structured Settlement

Although most damage awards are paid in a lump sum by the insurance carrier, structured settlements have become a more attractive alternative to the insurance carrier. The structured settlement is usually used when the recovery is significant and the paying party is financially unable to make a lump sum payment, or in cases involving minors. Generally, the plaintiff receives payments from a trust or annuity which is funded by the defendant.

The structured settlement allows for the payment of money, in installments, over a period of time. The first payment usually consists of a large lump sum, and the balance is paid out over a period of time during the life of the plaintiff. The installment payments are made according to the terms of a settlement agreement.

Some states have enacted legislation which permits the defendant to pay the award in installments in an effort to reduce the overall costs associated with paying a damage award—particularly very large awards.

Some legislation provides that the payments cease upon the death of the plaintiff—whether or not the amount has been paid in full—a further benefit to the insurance carrier.

APPENDIX 1
DIRECTORY OF STATE PHYSICIAN
LICENSING BUREAUS

STATE	NAME	ADDRESS	TELEPHONE
Alabama	Alabama State Board of Medical Examiners	P.O. Box 946, Montgomery, Alabama 36102	205-832-6890
Alaska	Alaska Board of Medical Examiners	Pouch D, Juneau, Alaska 99811	907-465-2541
Arizona	Arizona State Board of Medical Examiners	5060 North Nineteenth Avenue, Suite 300, Phoenix, Arizona 85015	602-255-3751
Arkansas	Arkansas State Medical Board	P.O. Box 102, Harrisburg, Arkansas 72432	501-578-2677
California	California Board of Medical Quality Assurance	1340 Howe Avenue, Sacramento, California 95825	916-920-6411
Colorado	Colorado Board of Medical Examiners	132 State Services Building, 1525 Sherman Street Denver, Colorado 80203	303-866-2468
Connecticut	Connecticut Medical Examining Board	79 Elm Street, Hartford, Connecticut 06115	203-566-5630
Delaware	Delaware Board of Medical Practice	Margaret O'Neill Building, P.O. Box 1401, Dover, Delaware 19901	302-763-4753
District of Columbia	District of Columbia Commission on Licensure to Practice the Healing Art	605 G Street N.W., Washington, DC 20001	202-727-5365

STATE	NAME	ADDRESS	TELEPHONE
Florida	Florida Board of Medical Examiners	130 North Monroe Street Tallahassee, Florida 32301	904-488-0595
Georgia	Georgia Composite Board of Medical Examiners	166 Pryor Street, Southwest Atlanta, Georgia 30303	404-656-7067
Hawaii	Hawaii Board of Medical Examiners	P.O. Box 3469, Honolulu, Hawaii 96801	808-548-4100
Idaho	Idaho State Board of Medicine	700 West State Street, Boise, Idaho 83720	208-334-2822
Illinois	Professional Regulation	106 West Randolph, Chicago, Illinois 60601	312-917-4500
Indiana	Medical Licensing Board of Indiana	One American Square, Suite 1020, P.O. Box 82067, Indianapolis, Indiana 46282	317-232-2960
Iowa	Iowa State Board of Medical Examiners	State Capitol Complex, Executive Hills West, Des Moiner Iowa 50319	515-281-5171
Kansas	Kansas State Board of Healing Arts	503 Kansas Avenue, Suite 500, Topeka, Kansas 66534	913-296-7413
Kentucky	Kentucky State Board of Medical Licensure	3532 Ephraim Drive, Louisville, Kentucky 40205	502-456-2220
Louisiana	Louisiana State Board of Medical Examiners	830 Union Street, Suite 100, New Orleans, Louisiana 70112	504-524-6763
Maine	Maine State Board of Registration in Medicine	RFD #3, Box 461, Waterville, Maine 04901	207-873-2184
Maryland	Maryland Board of Medical Examiners	201 West Preston Street, Baltimore, Maryland 21201	301-383-2020

STATE	NAME	ADDRESS	TELEPHONE
Massachusetts	Massachusetts Board of Registration in Medicine	Room 1511, Leverett Saltonstall Building, 100 Cambridge Street, Boston, Massachusetts 02202	617-727-9446
Michigan	Michigan Board of Medicine	905 Southland, P.O. Box 3001, Lansing, Michigan 48909	517-373-0680
Minnesota	Minnesota State Board of Medical Examiners	717 Delaware Street S.E., Suite 352, Minneapolis, Minnesota 55414	612-296-5534
Mississippi	Mississippi State Board of Medical Licensure	P.O. Box 1700, Jackson, Mississippi 39205	601-354-6645
Missouri	Missouri State Board of Registration for the Healing Arts	P.O. Box 4, Jefferson City, Missouri 65102	314-751-2334
Montana	Montana State Board of Medical Examiners	1424 9th Avenue, Helena, Montana 59620	406-449-3737
Nebraska	Nebraska Bureau of Examining Boards	P.O. Box 95007, Lincoln, Nebraska 68509	402-471-2115
Nevada	Nevada State Board of Medical Examiners	P.O. Box 7238, Reno, Nevada 89510	702-329-2559
New Hampshire	New Hampshire Board of Registration in Medicine	Health and Welfare Building Hazen Drive, Concord, New Hampshire 03301	603-271-4502
New Jersey	New Jersey State Board of Medical Examiners	28 West State Street, Room 914, Trenton, New Jersey 08608	609-292-4843
New Mexico	New Mexico State Board of Medical Examiners	227 E. Palace Avenue, Santa Fe, New Mexico 87501	505-827-2215

STATE	NAME	ADDRESS	TELEPHONE
New York	New York Department of Health Office of Professional Medical Conduct	Empire State Plaza, Tower Building, Albany, New York 12237	518-474-8537
North Carolina	North Carolina State Board of Medical Examiners	222 North Person Street, Suite 214, Raleigh, North Carolina 27601	919-833-5321
North Dakota	North Dakota Board of Medical Examiners	418 East Rosser Avenue, Bismarck, North Dakota 58501	701-233-9485
Ohio	Ohio State Medical Board	65 South Front Street, Suite 510, Columbus, Ohio 43215	614-466-3934
Oklahoma	Oklahoma State Board of Medical Examiners	P.O. Box 18256, Oklahoma City, Oklahoma 73154	405-848-6841
Oregon	Oregon Board of Medical Examiners	1002 Loyalty Building, 317 S.W. Alder Street, Portland, Oregon 97204	503-229-5770
Pennsylvania	Pennsylvania Board of Medical Education and Licensure	P.O. Box 2649, Harrisburg, Pennsylvania 17105	717-787-2381
Rhode Island	Rhode Island Department of Health	104 Cannon Building, 75 Davis Street, Providence, Rhode Island 02908	401-277-2827
South Carolina	South Carolina State Board of Medical Examiners	1315 Blanding Street, Columbia, South Carolina 29201	803-758-3361
South Dakota	South Dakota State Board of Medical and Osteopathic Examiners	608 West Avenue, North Sioux Falls, South Dakota 57104	605-336-1965

STATE	NAME	ADDRESS	TELEPHONE
Tennessee	Tennessee State Board of Medical Examiners	320 R.S. Gass State Office Building, Ben Allen Road, Nashville, Tennessee 37216	615-741-7280
Texas	Texas State Board of Medical Examiners	P.O. Box 13562, Capitol Station, Austin, Texas 78711	512-305-7010
Utah	Utah Department of Registration	State Office Building, Room 5000, Salt Lake City, Utah 84114	801-268-6242
Vermont	Vermont State Board of Medicine	109 State Street, Montpelier, Vermont 05602	802-828-2363

APPENDIX 2:
DIRECTORY OF STATE LICENSING AGENCIES FOR MEDICAL FACILITIES

STATE	NAME	DEPARTMENT	ADDRESS	TELEPHONE
Alabama	Alabama Department of Public Health	Health Facility Licensure and Certification	State Office Building, Montgomery, Alabama 36130	205-832-3253
Alaska	Department of Health and Social Services	Division of Public Health	Pouch H-06, Juneau, Alaska 99811	907-465-3090
Arizona	Department of Health	Health Facility Licensure and Certification	1740 West Adams Street, Phoenix, Arizona 85007	602-255-1118
Arkansas	Department of Health	Health Facility Services	4815 West Markham Street, Little Rock, Arkansas 72201	501-661-2201
California	Department of Health Services	Health Facilities Licensure and Certification	744 P Street, Sacramento, California 95814	916-445-3281
Colorado	Department of Health	Health Facility Licensure and Certification	4210 East Eleventh Avenue, Denver, Colorado 80220	303-320-8333

STATE	NAME	DEPARTMENT	ADDRESS	TELEPHONE
Connecticut	Department of Health Services	Hospital and Medical Care Services	79 Elm Street, Hartford, Connecticut 06115	203-566-3985
Delaware	Department of Health and Social Services	Health Facility Licensure and Certification	Jesse S. Cooper Memorial Building Dover, Delaware 19901	302-995-6674
District of Columbia	Department of Human Services	Health Facility Licensure and Certification	1875 Connecticut Avenue N.W., Washington, DC 20009	202-727-2009
Florida	Department of Health and Rehabilitative Services	Health Facility Licensure and Certification	1323 Winewood Boulevard, Tallahassee, Florida 32301	904-359-6022
Georgia	Department of Human Resources	Licensing and Certification	Atlanta, Georgia 30334	404-894-5144
Hawaii	Department of Health	Health Facility Licensure and Certification	Kinau Hale, P.O. Box 337, 8honolulu, Hawaii 96801	808-548-6510
Idaho	Department of Health and Welfare Division of Health	Health Facility Licensure and Certification	Statehouse Mail, Boise, Idaho 83720	208-334-4172
Illinois	Department of Public Health	Division of Health Facility Standards	525 West Jefferson, Springfield, Illinois 62761	217-782-7412
Indiana	Indiana State Board of Health	Health Facility Licensure and Certification	1330 West Michigan Street, P.O. Box 1964, Indianapolis, Indiana 46206	317-633-8442

STATE	NAME	DEPARTMENT	ADDRESS	TELEPHONE
Iowa	Department of Health	Health Facility Licensure and Certification	Lucas State Office Building, Des Moines, Iowa 50319	515-281-4125
Kansas	Department of Health and Environment	Health Facility Licensure and Certification	Forbes Field, Topeka, Kansas 66620	913-862-9360
Kentucky	Department of Human Resources	Ombudsman	275 Main Street, Frankfort, Kentucky 40621	502-564-5497
Louisiana	Department of Health and Human Resources	Office of Licensing and Regulations	P.O. Box 60630, New Orleans, Louisiana 70160	504-342-6721
Maine	Department of Human Services	Health Facility Licensure and Certification	Augusta, Maine 04333	207-289-2606
Maryland	Department of Health and Mental Hygiene	Licensing and Certification	201 West Preston Street, Baltimore, Maryland 21201	301-383-2517
Massachusetts	Office of Human Services	Health Facilities	600 Washington Street, Boston, Massachusetts 02111	617-727-6240
Michigan	Department of Public Health	Health Facility Licensing and Certification	3500 North Logan Street, Lansing, Michigan 48909	517-373-0900
Minnesota	Department of Health	Health Facility Licensure and Certification	717 Delaware Street S.E., Minneapolis, Minnesota 55440	612-296-5420

STATE	NAME	DEPARTMENT	ADDRESS	TELEPHONE
Mississippi	Health Care Commission	Health Facility Licensing and Certification	26, Insurance Center Drive, Jackson, Mississippi 39201	601-981-6880
Missouri	Missouri Division of Health	Hospital Licensure and Certification	Broadway State Office Building, P.O. Box 570, Jefferson City, Missouri 65101	314-751-2713
Montana	Department of Health and Environmental Sciences	Health Facility Licensure and Certification	Cogswell Building, Helena, Montana 59620	406-449-2037
Nebraska	Department of Health	Health Facility Licensure and Certification	301 Centennial Mall South, Lincoln, Nebraska 68509	402-471-2105
Nevada	Department of Human Resources	Health Facility Licensure and Certification	505 East King Street—Capitol Complex, Carson City, Nevada 89710	702-884-4475
New Hampshire	Division of Public Health Services	Health Facility Licensure and Certification	Health and Welfare Building Hazen Drive, Concord, New Hampshire 03301	603-271-4592
New Jersey	Department of Health	Health Facility Licensure and Certification	CN 360, John Fitch Plaza, Trenton, New Jersey 08625	609-292-5764
New Mexico	Health and Environment Department	Bureau of Health Facilities	P.O. Box 968, Santa Fe, New Mexico 87504	505-827-2745

STATE	NAME	DEPARTMENT	ADDRESS	TELEPHONE
New York	Department of Health Bureau of Project Management	Division of Health Facility Planning	Corning Tower, Suite 9-300, Empire State Plaza, Albany, New York 12237	518-473-4119
North Carolina	Department of Human Resources Division of Health Services	Health Facility Licensure and Certification	P.O. Box 2091, Raleigh, North Carolina 27602	919-733-2342
North Dakota	State Department of Health	Health Facility Licensure and Certification	State Capitol, Bismarck, North Dakota 58505	701-224-2352
Ohio	Department of Health	Health Facility Licensure and Certification	P.O. Box 118, Columbus, Ohio 43216	614-466-7857
Oklahoma	State Department of Health	Health Facilities Service	P.O. Box 53551, Oklahoma City, Oklahoma 73152	405-271-5114
Oregon	Department of Human Resources	Health Facility Licensure and Certification	P.O. Box 231, Portland, Oregon 97207	503-229-5686
Pennsylvania	Department of Health	Hospital Licensing	P.O. Box 90, Harrisburg, Pennsylvania 17120	717-783-8980
Rhode Island	Department of Health	Facility Regulation	75 Davis Street, Providence, Rhode Island 02908	401-277-2566
South Carolina	Department of Health and Environ-mental Con-trol	Health Facility Licensing and Certification	2600 Bull Street, Columbia, South Carolina 29201	803-758-4567

STATE	NAME	DEPARTMENT	ADDRESS	TELEPHONE
South Dakota	Department of Health	Health Facility Licensure and Certification	Joe Foss Building, Pierre, South Dakota 57501	605-773-3364
Tennessee	Department of Public Health	Health Facility Licensure and Certification	Cordell Hull Building, Nashville, Tennessee 37219	615-741-6379
Texas	Department of Health	Bureau of Licensing and Certification	1100 West 49th Street, Austin, Texas 78756	512-458-7538
Utah	Utah Department of Health	Health Facility Licensure and Certification	150 West North Temple, P.O. Box 2500, Salt Lake City, Utah 84110	801-533-7016
Vermont	Department of Health	Health Facility Licensure and Certification	60 Main Street, Burlington, Vermont 05401	802-862-5701
Virginia	State Health Department	Health Facility Licensing and Certification	109 Governor Street, Richmond, Virginia 23219	804-786-2081
Washington	Department of Social and Health Services	Health Facility Licensure and Certification	Mail Stop LJ-18, Olympia, Washington 98504	206-753-5851

APPENDIX 3:
SAMPLE DURABLE POWER OF ATTORNEY FOR HEALTH CARE

APPOINTMENT made this (enter date).

I, (Name and address), being of sound mind, willfully and voluntarily appoint (name, address, city, state, phone), as my Health Care Agent (hereinafter "Agent") with a Durable Power of Attorney to make any and all health care decisions for me, except to the extent stated otherwise in this document.

EFFECTIVE DATE

This Durable Power of Attorney and Appointment of Health Care Agent shall take effect at such time as I become comatose, incapacitated, or otherwise mentally or physically incapable of giving directions or consent regarding the use of life-sustaining procedures or any other health care measures.

"Health care" in this context means any treatment, service, or procedure utilized to maintain, diagnose, or treat any physical or mental condition.

DETERMINATION OF MEDICAL CONDITION

A determination of incapacity shall be certified by my attending physician and by a second physician who is neither employed by the facility where I am a patient nor associated in practice with my attending physician and who shall be appointed to independently assess and evaluate my capacity by the appropriate administrator of the facility where I am a patient.

AUTHORITY OF HEALTH CARE AGENT

My Agent is authorized, in consultation with my attending physician, to direct the withdrawal or withholding of any life-sustaining procedures, as defined herein, as (he or she) solely in the exercise of (his or her) judgment shall determine are appropriate to give comply with my wishes and desires.

In addition, my Agent by acceptance of this Appointment agrees and is hereby directed to use (his or her) best efforts to make those decisions that I would make in the exercise of my right to refuse treatment and not those that (he or she) or others might believe to be in my best interests.

APPOINTMENT OF ALTERNATE AGENTS

If the person designated as my Agent is unable or unwilling to accept this Appointment, I designate the following persons to serve as my Agent to make health care decisions for me as authorized by this document. They shall serve in the following order:

1. First Alternate Agent: (name, address and telephone)

2. Second Alternate Agent: (name, address and telephone)

DURATION

I understand that this Power of Attorney exists indefinitely unless I define a shorter time herein or execute a revocation. If I am incapacitated at such time as this Power of Attorney expires (if applicable), the authority I have granted my Agent shall continue until such time as I am capable of giving directions regarding my health care.

(If applicable:) This power of attorney ends on the following date:

COPIES AND DISTRIBUTION

The original of this document is kept at (address where kept). I have made (#) copies of this document. Numbered and signed copies have been provided to the following individuals or institutions: (List names, addresses and phone numbers of individuals and institutions).

STATEMENT OF WITNESSES

I state this (enter date), under penalty of perjury, that the Declarant has identified (himself or herself) to me and that the Declarant signed or acknowledged this Durable Power of Attorney and Appointment of Health Care Agent in my presence.

I believe the Declarant to be of sound mind, and the Declarant has affirmed (his or her) awareness of the nature of this document and is signing it voluntarily and free from duress. The Declarant requested that I serve as a witness to (his or her) execution of this document.

I am not the person appointed as Agent by this document, and I am not a provider of health or residential care, an employee of a provider of health or residential care, the operator of a community care facility, or an employee of an operator of a health care facility.

I declare that I am not related to the Declarant by blood, marriage, or adoption and that to the best of my knowledge I am not entitled to any part of the estate of the Declarant on the death of the principal under a will or by operation of law.

I declare that I have no claim against any portion of the estate of the Declarant upon (his or her) death, nor any personal financial responsibility for the payment of Declarant's medical bills or any other of Declarant's obligations.

Signature Line of Witness #1

Address of Witness #1

Signature Line of Witness #2

Address of Witness #2

Signature Line of Witness #3

Address of Witness #3

Subscribed and acknowledged before me by the Declarant, (Name), and by his or her witnesses (Names) on (enter date).

Notary Signature and Stamp

APPENDIX 4:
RELEASE FROM LIABILITY

We, the undersigned, are the family of [name of patient] . [His or her] attending physician [name of physician] has advised that [patient] has suffered severe and irreversible brain injury that precludes any cognitive, meaningful or functional future existence. [Note: Or set forth a similar statement of the patient's condition].

We understand that [his or her] current survival is contingent upon [insert the procedure to be withheld or withdrawn]. It is our desire and that of the patient as expressed in [his or her] Living Will, Health Care Declaration, Durable Power of Attorney, and/or Appointment of Health Care Agent executed on [date[s]], that all "life-sustaining procedures" as therein defined be discontinued.

By [my or our] signature(s), we hereby release and agree to hold harmless [his or her] physicians and the nurses and staff of [name of facility], from any liability, claims for damages, or causes of action that might otherwise be brought as a result of the death that likely will occur subsequent to the discontinuance of the above-described life-sustaining procedures.

[Insert Date]

BY: [Insert signature line for Name/Address of Guardian, Next of Kin, Proxy or Surrogate as Releasor]

[State relationship to patient]

BY: [Witness #1]

[Insert Date]

BY: [Witness #1]

[Insert Date]

Subscribed and acknowledged before me by the Releasor [Insert Name of Releasor], and by [Insert Names of Witnesses], witnesses, this   day of   ,
20

[Notary Stamp]

APPENDIX 5:
TABLE OF POSSIBLE COMPLICATIONS ASSOCIATED WITH COMMON MEDICAL PROCEDURES

NAME OF PROCEDURE	POSSIBLE COMPLICATIONS
1. Adenoidectomy	Bleeding, Nasal speech, Nasal regurgitation of food or liquids
2. Anesthesia, general	Abnormal reaction to drugs, Aspiration of stomach contents, Injury to vocal cords or throat, Injury to teeth, lips, and tongue, Brain damage, Malignant hyperthermia
3. Angiography, cerebral	injury to the arteries entered, Bleeding at the site of entry by catheter, Stroke, Blindness or brain damage, Emboli to the brain, Allergic reaction to the injected contrast medium
4. Angiography, coronary	Injury to the artery, Damage to heart, myocardial infarction, Possible need for open heart surgery, Irregular heartbeat, Bleeding at the site of entrance, Allergic reaction to injected contrast medium
5. Angioplasty	Paraplegia, Loss of extremity, Bowel infarction, Renal failure
6. Aortic Dissection	Stroke, Renal failure, Bowel infarction, Paraplegia, Death
7. Aortic Graft	Bleeding or Infection, Infection or emboli, Kidney failure or loss of limb, Inadequate blood to bowel or spinal cord, Myocardial infarction, Sexual dysfunction, Death

NAME OF PROCEDURE	POSSIBLE COMPLICATIONS
8. Appendectomy	Infection, Bleeding, Intra-abdominal abscess, Leakage from the colon requiring colostomy, Hernia in the incision
9. Arteriovenous Shunt for Hemodialysis	Bleeding or infection, Damage blood vessel with risk of rupture, Recurrent thrombosis, Severe edema of extremity, Inadequate blood supply to extremity, Inadequate blood supply to nerves
10. Birth of child	Injury to bladder, Injury to rectum, Fistula between vagina and rectum, Hemorrhage possibly requiring hysterectomy, Brain damage to fetus
11. Blood Transfusion	Fever, Kidney failure, Heart failure, Hepatitis, Aids
12. Breast Augmentation	Risks of use of silicon gel are excluded, Scar formation around implant causing hard breast, Deflation of implant, Loss of sensation to the nipple and breast, Persistent pain in breast, Distortion of breast mound, Leakage of implant contents
13. Breast Biopsy, Excisional	Infection and/or blood clot, Failure to obtain accurate diagnosis, Disfiguring scar, Failure to locate and remove abnormality
14. Cardiopulmonary Bypass	Stroke, Respiratory complications, Kidney failure, Death
15. Carotid Endarterectomy	Blood clots, Infection, Stroke, Nerve injury causing mouth, throat, or tongue problems, Myocardial infarction, Death
16. Cataract Surgery	Loss of vision or decrease in vision, Loss of eye, Bleeding inside or behind eye, Painful eye, Droopy eyelid
17. Catheterization, central venous	Hemorrhage into chest cavity or elsewhere, Pericardial tamponade (compression of heart), Cardiac arrest or stroke, Collapse of lung, Damage to blood vessels, Infusion of fluid into chest cavity
18. Cervix Removal	Uncontrollable leakage of urine, Injury to the bladder, Injury to the bowel or intestinal obstruction, Injury to the ureter, Sterility, Pulmonary embolism

NAME OF PROCEDURE	POSSIBLE COMPLICATIONS
19. Cholecystectomy	Pancreatitis, Injury to the bile duct, Retained stones in the bile duct, Narrowing of the bile duct, Injury to the bowel
20. Coarctation of Aorta	Quadriplegia or paraplegia, Permanent hoarseness, Leakage of body fluid from intestines into chest, Loss of bowel and/or bladder function, Impotence in males
21. Colon Surgery	Infection of the incision, Intra-abdominal abscess, Leakage from colon and possible colostomy, Injury to other organs or blood vessels, Diarrhea—sometimes permanent, Formation of scar tissue causing intestinal blockage, Hernia in incision
22. Colonoscopy	Infection or bleeding, Perforation of colon or rectal wall, Cardiac arrhythmias
23. Dental Implants	Infection, bleeding, failure to heal, Permanent and disfiguring scarring, Premature loss of implant, or mobility, Loss of bone, Numbness of face or mouth, Fracture of jaw, Injury to adjacent teeth or sinus
24. Dilation and Curettage	Hemorrhage with possible hysterectomy, Perforation of the uterus, Injury to the bowel or bladder, Sterility
25. Ear Tubes	Persistent infection, Perforation of eardrum or cyst behind the eardrum, Need to surgically remove tubes
26. Endoscopic Retrograde Cholangio Pancreatogram (ERCP)	Infection, Perforation of esophagus, stomach, or intestines, Cardiac arrhythmias, Pancreatic inflammation
27. Endoscopy, abdominal	Puncture of the bowel or blood vessel, Abdominal infection, Operation to correct injury, Injury to ureter, Injury to bladder
28. Epidural, spinal	Abnormal reaction to drugs, Leakage of cerebrospinal fluid, Epidural blood clot or abscess, Broken needles or catheters, Incomplete analgesia, Back pain and/or paralysis, Severe headaches

NAME OF PROCEDURE	POSSIBLE COMPLICATIONS
29. Femoral Bypass Grafts	Bleeding requiring reoperation, Necrosis of skin around incision, Thrombi or emboli, Limb loss, Nerve damage, Myocardial infarction, Death
30. Fibroid Removal (Uterine myomectomy)	Uncontrollable leakage of urine, Injury to bladder, Injury to the ureter, Injury to the bowel and/or intestinal obstruction, Sterility, Pulmonary embolism
31. Gastrectomy or Phloroplasty	Infection of incision or inside abdomen, Bleeding requiring transfusion, Leakage from stomach, Inability to maintain weight, Chronic vomiting after eating, Diarrhea and need for vitamin B-12 injections, Recurrence of condition for which surgery was done
32. Hemodialysis	Hypotension, hemorrhage, sepsis, cardiac arrhythmias, Allergic reaction to tubing and dialyzer, Pulmonary edema, air bubbles in the bloodstream, seizure, hypothermia, fever, metabolic disorders, Viral infections such as HIV, Cardiac arrest
33. Hemorrhoidectomy	Bleeding, Post operative pain, especially with bowel movements, Temporary/permanent difficulty controlling bowels or gas, Recurrence of hemorrhoids, Narrowing of anal opening requiring repeated dialations
34. Hernia Repair, Infection	Bleeding, Recurrence of hernia, Injury to or loss of testicle or spermatic cords, Nerve injury resulting in numbness or chronic pain
35. Hysterectomy, abdominal or vaginal	Uncontrollable leakage of urine, Injury to bladder, Injury to ureter, Injury to the bowel and/or intestinal obstruction, Painful intercourse, Ovarian failure requiring hormone administration, Formation of fistula between vagina and rectum
36. Kidney Stone Lithotripsy	Bleeding in or around kidney, Obstruction of kidney by stone particles, Failure to completely fragment stones, High blood pressure, Loss of kidney

NAME OF PROCEDURE	POSSIBLE COMPLICATIONS
37. Liver Biopsy	Bleeding, Lung collapse, Internal leakage of bile, Puncture of other organs, Aspiration pheumonia
38. Lumpectomy	Infection or blood clot, Disfiguring scar, Fluid collection in arm pit, Numbness to arm, Swelling of arm, Damage to nerves of arm or chest, Recurrence of cancer
39. Mastectomy, radical	Limitation of movement of shoulder or arm, Swelling of the arm, Losss of skin requiring graft, Failure to eradicate the malignancy, Injury to major blood vessel
40. Oral Surgery	Infection, bleeding, failure to heal, Injury to adjacent teeth, Numbness of face and/or mouth, Fracture of either jaw, Opening between mouth and sinus or nose, Tooth fragment in sinus, Dry socket
41. Penile Implant	Bleeding and infection, Penile pain or numbness, Injury to bladder or urethra, Problems with implantable prosthetic
42. Prostatectomy	Bleeding and/or infection, Injury to bladder, urethra, or rectum, Impotence, Retrograde ejaculation, Bladder blockage, Incontinence
43. Radial Keratotomy	Loss of vision or decrease in vision, Loss of eye, Variable vision, Radiating images around lights, Over or under correction, Cataract formation, Retained need for glasses
44. Radiation Therapy, Head/neck- Initial Reaction	Altered sense of smell, taste, or nausea, Difficulty swallowing, weight loss, fatigue, Hoarseness, cough, loss of voice, Hearing loss, dizziness, Dry and irritable eyes, Increased risk of infection and/or bleeding, Intensified by chemotherapy
45. Radiation Therapy, head/neck-Late Reaction	Tooth decay and gum changes, Bone damage in jaws, Hair loss, scarring of skin, Swelling of tissues under chin, Brain, spinal cord or nerve damage, Pituitary or thyroid gland damage, Second cancers developing

NAME OF PROCEDURE	POSSIBLE COMPLICATIONS
46. Radiation Therapy, Thorax-Initial Reaction	Skin changes, hair loss on the chest, Inflammation of the esophagus, heart sac, or lungs, Bleeding or fistula from tumor destruction, Intermittent electric shock-like feeling in the lower body, Increased risk of infection or bleeding, Intensified by chemotherapy
47. Radiation Therapy, Thorax-Late Reaction	Changes in skin texture, scarring, hair loss, Lung scarring or shrinkage, Narrowing of esophagus, Constriction of heart sac, Damage to heart muscle or arteries, Fracture of ribs, Spinal cord or liver damage
48. Radical Mastectomy	Limitation of shoulder or arm movement, Swelling of the arm, Loss of the skin of the chest, Failure to completely eradicate the malignancy, Decreased sensation or numbness, Injury to major blood vessels
49. Renal Biopsy	Injury to adjacent organs, Infection, Hypotension, Bleeding from the kidney, Intestinal perforation
50. Rhinoplasty	Bleeding, Infection, Disappointing cosmetic result, Impaired breathing through nose, Septal perforation
50. Septoplasty	Bleeding, Infection, Injury to nerve of upper teeth, Septal perforation, Spinal fluid leak
51. Sigmoidoscopy/Protoscopy	Infection or bleeding, Perforation of colon or rectal wall, Cardiac arrhythmia
52. Sinus Surgery	Bleeding, Infection, Scar formation, Spinal fluid leak, Infection of brain tissue, Blindness or eye damage, Injury to sense of smell
53. Spinal Manipulation	Stroke, Disc herniation, Soft tissue injury, Rib fracture
54. Spinal operation	Pain, numbness or paralysis, Weakness in extremities, Loss of bladder function, Loss of bowel function, Unstable spine, Recurrence of condition, Injury to blood vessels

NAME OF PROCEDURE	POSSIBLE COMPLICATIONS
55. Thyroidectomy	Permanent hoarseness or impaired speech, Low blood calcium levels requiring extensive medication, Life long requirement of thyroid medication
56. Tonsillectomy	Bleeding, Injury to nerves to tongue, Nasal speech
57. Vasectomy	Bleeding and/or infection, Testicular swelling or pain, Spermatic Granuloma (nodule in cord at site of surgery), Reconnection of vas tube resulting in fertility
58. Ventriculoperitoneal Shunt	Heart failure, Infection in blood stream, Occlusion of large veins in chest, Blood or fluid collection around heart, Blood clots in the lung
59. Ventriculoperitoneal Shunt Placement	Malfunction of shunt due to infection, Collection of blood or fluid between brain and skull, Headaches, Development of need for another shunt, Blood clot in brain, Blindness, seizures or epilepsy, Leaks or separation of catheter

Source: The Association for Responsible Medicine.

NOTE: The risks listed below are taken from the rules of the Louisiana Department of Health and Hospitals. The risks were defined by the Louisiana Medical Disclosure Panel and are required to be disclosed by physicians to patients. The Louisiana Medical Disclosure Panel Law requires that physicians tell patients (1) the nature of the patient's condition (2) the general nature of the proposed treatment/surgery (3) the risks of the proposed treatment/surgery, as defined by the Panel, and (4) reasonable therapeutic alternatives and risks associated with such alternatives. ARM suggests patients discuss these risks with your doctors and ask how often the risks have occurred in his/her practice before undergoing any procedure.

APPENDIX 6:
SAMPLE INFORMED CONSENT
AGREEMENT

I, [name of patient] allow [name of physician] to perform upon me an operation known as [type of operation to be performed, e.g., appendectomy, mastectomy, etc.]. I further understand that he/she may be assisted in performing this operation by [list any assisting physicians, if applicable], but that the operation will be primarily performed by [name of physician].

I have been informed that [name of physician] has performed [#] [type of operation[s]] during the last 12 months and that the mortality rate was [xx%], the infection rate was [xx%] and the mistake rate was [xx%].

The hospital, [name of physician], has informed me that [#] related operations were performed during the last 12 months at this facility and that the mortality rate was [xx%], the infection rate was [xx%], and the mistake rate was [xx%].

Dr. [name of physician] and this hospital carry liability insurance in the amount of [$xxx] and [$xxx] respectively. This liability insurance is/is not approximately the same as other doctors and hospitals performing this operation would be expected to carry to provide compensation to patients who may die or be injured by medical mismanagement.

I have been informed that a [type of operation] is a major/minor operation and will be performed as described below:

[Describe in detail procedure to be performed as well as the physician's rights to perform further surgery if an unexpected condition is encountered during the course of the surgery].

As with any major surgery, bleeding can occur and at times can be serious. In addition, infection can occur and the risks of developing such an infection are as reported above. [Describe all further risks of the procedure in detail].

[Describe details of recovery period].

I have been advised that a [type of operation] is necessary because [provide details as to why the particular procedure is necessary].

I have been advised that the alternatives of treatment include [provide details of all alternative treatments available, including the possible outcome and risks associated with the alternative treatments].

I have been advised that it is the opinion of my doctor that a [type of operation] is indicated and the risks of the operation are less than the alternatives, and I have been given the opportunity of seeking independent consultation prior to having this surgery.

Although I have been fully informed about the risks of undergoing a [type of procedure], I am willing to undergo the operation. This does not relieve my doctor of any responsibilities for acts of negligence, which would include rendering substandard care to me, causing injuries which should not have occurred, even though I am aware that there may be a risk in having the operation performed. I agree to undergo a [type of operation] after being fully informed, but expect that proper care shall be rendered to me at all times. This includes post-operative care by my physicians and the nurses and hospital personnel.

Dated:

Signature Line for Patient

Dated: .

Signature Line for Doctor

APPENDIX 7:
STATE STATUTES OF LIMITATIONS IN MEDICAL MALPRACTICE CASES

ALABAMA [ALA. CODE § 6-5-482]

Action must be commenced within two years after the act or omission giving rise to the claim; provided, that if the cause of action is not discovered and could not reasonably have been discovered within the two-year period, then the action may be commenced within six months from the date of such discovery or the date of learning of facts that would reasonably lead to such discovery, whichever is earlier. Although this statute of limitations is subject to tolling for minority or disability, in no event may an action be brought more than four years after the act or omission, except that a minor who is under the age of four at the time of the act or omission accrues has until his eighth birthday to commence an action.

ALASKA [ALASKA STAT. § 09.10.070; § 09.10.140]

Action must be commenced within two years. If the claimant is under the age of majority, or incompetent by reason of mental illness or disability, at the time the cause of action accrues, the statute begins to run when the disability is lifted, but this cannot extend the period for more than two years after the disability ceases.

ARIZONA [ARIZ. REV. STAT. ANN. § 12-542; § 12-502]

Action must be commenced within two years after the cause of action accrues. The statute of limitations is tolled if a claimant is under eighteen years of age, mentally incompetent, or imprisoned.

ARKANSAS [ARK. CODE ANN. § 16-114-203]

Action must be commenced within two years after the date of the wrongful act complained of. However, if the action is based upon the discovery of a foreign object, the action may be brought within one year from the date of discovery or the date when the object should have been discovered, whichever is earlier. If an individual is nine years old or younger at the time of the act or omission complained of, he has until his eleventh birthday to commence an action, and if the injury could not reasonably be known by then, he has until the later of his nineteenth birthday or two years after the injury is discovered or reasonably could have been discovered.

CALIFORNIA [CAL. CIV. PROC. CODE § 340.5]

Action must be commenced within one year from the date the claimant discovered the negligent act, but no more than three years from the date of injury. For retained foreign body cases, the statute is tolled until the claimant discovers or should have discovered the injury. Actions by or on behalf of minors must be brought within three years from the date of the negligent act, unless the child is under the age of six, in which case the action must be commenced within three years or prior to the child's eighth birthday, whichever provides the longer time period.

COLORADO [COLO. REV. STAT. ANN. §§ 13-80-102.5 AND 13-80-108; § 13-80-102.5]

Action must be commenced within two years after the date the injury and its cause were known or should have been known with the exercise of reasonable diligence. In no event may a medical malpractice action be brought more than three years after the act or omission that gave rise to the action, unless the malpractice was knowingly concealed, the act or omission consisted of leaving an unauthorized foreign object in the body of the claimant, or both the physical injury and its cause are not known or could not have been known through the exercise of reasonable diligence. A minor has at least until his eighth birthday to file.

CONNECTICUT [CONN. GEN. STAT. ANN. § 52-584]

Action must be commenced within two years from the date when the injury is first sustained or discovered or in the exercise of reasonable care should have been discovered, except that no such action may be brought more than three years from the date of the act or omission complained of.

DELAWARE [DEL. CODE ANN. TIT. 18, § 6856]

Action must be commenced within two years after the date of the injury. If, however, the injury is not one that can be discovered with reasonable diligence, the claimant is afforded an additional year in which to bring an action. For minors six years of age or younger, a medical malpractice action must be brought within the two-year time limit or by the child's sixth birthday, whichever is later.

DISTRICT OF COLUMBIA [D.C. CODE ANN. § 12-301; § 12-302]

Action must be commenced within three years from the time plaintiff knows or with the exercise of due diligence should know of the injury. Claimants who are either under the age of eighteen, mentally incompetent, or imprisoned may bring their action within three years following the removal of their disability.

FLORIDA [FLA. STAT. ANN. § 95.11(4)(B)]

Action must be commenced within two years from the date of the incident or from the date when the incident was or should have been discovered. In no event may an action be commenced more than four years after the incident giving rise to the action, except that this four-year period will not bar an action before the claimant's eighth birthday.

GEORGIA [GA. CODE ANN. § 9-3-71; § 9-3-72; § 9-3-73]

Action must be commenced within two years from the date of injury or death. Foreign object cases, however, may be brought any time within one year of discovering the object. These limits apply to minors, except that the statute of limitations will never run prior to the claimant's seventh birthday and the statute of repose will never run until the claimant's tenth birthday.

HAWAII [HAW. REV. STAT. § 657-7.3]

Action must be commenced within two years of the time the claimant discovers or reasonably should have discovered the injury.

Actions on behalf of minors must be commenced within six years from the date of the wrongful act, unless the child is under the age of ten, in which case the action need only be commenced within six years from the date of injury or by the child's tenth birthday, whichever is later.

IDAHO [IDAHO CODE § 5-210(4)]

Action must be commenced within two years from the time the cause of action accrued. However, when the action concerns a foreign object, the cause of action accrues when the injured party knows or should have known of the injury, and the action may be commenced within two years of the act complained of or one year following the date of accrual, whichever is later.

ILLINOIS [735 ILL. COMP. STAT. ANN. § 5/13-212]

Action must be commenced within two years from the date the claimant knew or reasonably should have known of the injury. If the claimant was under the age of eight when the cause of action accrued, the limitation period for filing suit is eight years from the date of the alleged negligence. In no event may a lawsuit be filed after the minor claimant's twenty-second birthday.

INDIANA [IND. CODE ANN. § 34-18-7-1]

Action must be commenced within two years from the date of the alleged act, omission, or neglect. A minor under the age of six years has until his eighth birthday to file.

IOWA [IOWA CODE ANN. § 614.1(9); § 614.8]

Action must be commenced within two years after the date upon which the claimant knew or reasonably should have known of the injury or death. Iowa Code Ann. § 614.1(9) No such action, however, may be brought more than six years after the date upon which the alleged wrongful act occurred, unless the action involves a retained foreign object. With respect to minors and mentally ill persons, Iowa extends the statutory period to one year from the date that the disability is removed.

KANSAS [KAN. STAT. ANN. § 60-513(7)(C); § 60-155]

Action must be commenced within two years from the date of the injury or from the date when the injury becomes reasonably ascertainable to the injured person. If a claimant is incompetent due to minority, incapacity, or imprisonment, he may bring an action within one year from the date the disability is removed.

KENTUCKY [KY. REV. STAT. ANN. § 413.140; § 413.170]

Action must be commenced within one year from the time the injury was or reasonably should have been discovered. The statute of limitations does not begin to run against a minor or person of unsound mind until the disability is lifted.

LOUISIANA [LA. REV. STAT. ANN. § 9:5628]

Action must be commenced within one year from the date of the alleged act, omission, or neglect, or within one year from the date of discovery of the alleged act, omission, or neglect.

MAINE [ME. REV. STAT. ANN. TIT. 24 § 2902]

Action must be commenced within three years from the date of the alleged negligent act or omission. With respect to foreign object cases, the action does not accrue until the injury is discovered or reasonably should have been discovered. Actions on behalf of minors must be brought within six years of the date of the alleged act or omission or within three years after the minor reaches the age of majority, whichever comes first.

MARYLAND [MD. CODE ANN., CTS. & JUD. PROC. § 5-109]

Action must be commenced within five years from the date when the injury was committed or three years from the date when the injury was discovered, whichever is earlier. Against a minor, the statute does not begin to run until a claimant has reached the age of eleven, and if the action involves a foreign object or injury to the reproductive system, the statute does not begin to run until the claimant is sixteen.

MASSACHUSETTS [MASS. ANN. LAWS CH. 260, § 4; CH. 231 § 60D]]

Action must be commenced within three years after the cause of action accrued, but in no event more than seven years after the alleged act or omission occurred, except in the case of foreign object actions. The statute of limitations for minors is the same as that for adults, except that a claim accruing on behalf of a child under six can always be brought before the child's ninth birthday.

MICHIGAN [MICH. COMP. LAWS ANN. § 600.5805(4); § 600.5838(A)

Action must be commenced within the longer of two years from the date of the act or omission giving rise to the claim or six months from the date the claimant discovers or should have discovered the existence of the claim. A claimant less than eight years old may file any time before his tenth birthday, and a claimant less than thirteen years old whose claim involves damage to the reproductive system may file any time before his fifteenth birthday.

MINNESOTA [MINN. STAT. ANN. § 541.07; § 541.15]

Action must be commenced within two years from the date the cause of action accrued. An infant's claim must be asserted within seven years from the date of the occurrence, or one year after the claimant reaches the age of majority, whichever period is shorter.

MISSISSIPPI [MISS. CODE ANN. § 15-1-36]

Action must be commenced within two years from the date the alleged act, omission, or neglect with reasonable diligence might have been first known or discovered. If the date the foregoing statute of limitations begins to run falls before a child's sixth birthday, an action may be brought within two years of the child's sixth birthday or two years after the child dies, whichever is first.

MISSOURI [MO. ANN. STAT. § 516.105]

Action must be commenced within two years from the date of the occurrence. However, if the claim involves a foreign object, the claimant is allowed two years from the date of discovering the alleged negligence to bring an action, but in no case shall an action for medical malpractice be brought more than ten years from the date of the alleged act. A minor under the age of ten has until his twelfth birthday to bring a cause of action.

MONTANA [MONT. CODE ANN. § 27-2-205(1)

Action must be commenced within three years from the date of injury or from the date when the claimant discovered the injury. The period is tolled for claimants whose injuries occurred while they were under the age of four years until they are eight years old or until they die, whichever date is earlier, and during any period in which the minor does not reside with a parent or guardian.

NEBRASKA [NEB. REV. STAT. § 25-222; § 44-2828]

Action must be commenced within two years after the act or omission that provides the basis for the action, or within one year after the claimant discovered the act or omission or discovered facts that should reasonably have led to such discovery. If the claimant is, at the time the cause of action accrues, under the age of 21 or suffering from a mental disorder, the limitations period does not begin to run until the disability is removed.

NEVADA [NEV. REV. STAT. ANN. § 41A.097]

Action must be commenced within four years from the date of injury, or two years from the date the injury was or should have been discovered, whichever is earlier. Parents or guardians of a minor claimant are governed by the above-noted period. However, in actions involving brain damage or birth defects, the limitation is extended until the child reaches ten years of age.

NEW HAMPSHIRE [N.H. REV. STAT. ANN. § 508:4; § 508:8]

Action must be commenced within three years, and if the injury was not and could not reasonably have been discovered at the time of the act or omission, this statute runs from the time plaintiff discovers or should have discovered the injury and its causal relationship to the act or omission complained of. An infant or mentally incompetent person has two years from the removal of the disability in which to sue.

NEW JERSEY [N.J. STAT. ANN. § 2A:14-2; § 2A:14-21]

Action must be commenced within two years from the date the cause of action accrued. If, at the time the cause of action accrued, the claimant was under the age of 21 or insane, the time does not begin to run until the disability is removed.

NEW MEXICO [N.M. STAT. ANN. § 41-5-13]

Action must be commenced within three years from the date when the alleged malpractice occurred. A minor under the age of six has until his ninth birthday to bring a medical malpractice action.

NEW YORK [N.Y.C.P.L.R. § 214A; § 208]

Action must be commenced within two and a half years from the act or omission complained of or from the end of a continuous treatment during which the act or omission took place. However, foreign object cases may be brought within one year from the date upon which the foreign object is discovered. A claimant's incompetency (*i.e.*, infancy or insanity) tolls the above-noted limitations until the disability ceases, but in medical malpractice cases this can only extend the limitations period a maximum of ten years.

NORTH CAROLINA [N.C. GEN. STAT. § 1-15; § 1-52(16); § 1-17]

Action must be commenced within three years from the date of the last act of the defendant giving rise to the cause of action or within one year of the date when the injury was or should have been discovered, but not more than four years from the date of the last act of defendant giving rise to the cause of action. Foreign object cases must be brought within one year from the date of discovery, but no longer than ten years from the date of the occurrence. For malpractice actions on behalf of minors, the same rules apply, except the child's action may also be brought any time before the child's nineteenth birthday.

NORTH DAKOTA [N.D. CENT. CODE § 28-01-18; § 28-01-25]

Action must be commenced within two years from the date the cause of action accrued. Discovery rule extends the period of limitations to two years from the date the injury was or should have been discovered, however no action can be brought more than six years after the date of injury. If the claimant is a minor, insane, or imprisoned when the cause of action accrues, the statute is tolled during the period of disability.

OHIO [OHIO REV. CODE ANN. § 2305.11(B)]

Action must be commenced within one year after the cause of action accrues. If, at the time the cause of action accrues, the claimant is either a minor, of unsound mind, or imprisoned, the statute of limitations is tolled until the disability is removed.

OKLAHOMA [OKLA. STAT. ANN. TIT. 76 § 18; TIT. 12; § 96]

Action must be commenced within two years from the date upon which the claimant knew or should have known of the alleged injury. Claimants under the age of twelve must bring a medical malpractice action within seven years from the date the injury was inflicted.

OREGON [OR. REV. STAT. § 12.110(4); §12.160]

Action must be commenced within two years from the date the injury is first discovered or in the exercise of reasonable care should have been discovered; however, no action may be brought more than five years from the date of treatment. The statute is tolled during the time a claimant is within 18 years of age or insane.

PENNSYLVANIA [42 PA. CONS. STAT. ANN. § 5524; § 5533]

Action must be commenced within two years. If the claimant is an unemancipated minor at the time the cause of action accrues, he may bring the action within two years after he reaches the age of eighteen.

RHODE ISLAND [R.I. GEN. LAWS § 9-1-14.1; § 10-7-2]

Action must be commenced within three years of the date of the incident, the date of death, or the date when the claimant knew or should have known of the wrongful act. With respect to minors and mentally incompetent persons, Rhode Island provides a three-year limitation period following removal of the disability.

SOUTH CAROLINA [S.C. CODE ANN. § 15-3-545]

Action must be commenced within three years from the date of the occurrence or the date when the occurrence should have been discovered, but in no case more than six years from the date of the occurrence. Foreign object cases may be brought within two years from the date of discovery. The statute of limitations is tolled during the claimant's minority; however, the period may not extend beyond seven years from the date of the occurrence, or more than one year after the child attains the age of majority, whichever period is shorter.

SOUTH DAKOTA [S.D. CODIFIED LAWS. ANN. § 15-2-14.1; § 15-2-22]

Action must be commenced within two years from the date the alleged malpractice occurred. The failure to remove a foreign object is a continuing tort for which the limitations period cannot begin until the end of treatment. Both minority and mental illness toll the statute, with restrictions. A claim can be brought within one year of the end of either disability, but this cannot be used in the case of mental illness to extend the period for bringing the action more than five years.

TENNESSEE [TENN. CODE ANN. § 29-26-116; § 28-1-106]

Action must be commenced within one year after the date upon which the claimant discovered the injury. However, no such action may be brought more than three years after the date on which the negligent act or omission occurred, unless the action involves a foreign object. If, at the time the cause of action accrues, the claimant is under the age of eighteen years or is of unsound mind, the claimant may bring an action within one year following the removal of the disability.

TEXAS [TEX. REV. CIV. STAT. ANN. ART. 4590I, § 10.01]

Action must be commenced within two years from the date of the breach or tort or from the completion of treatment. If the period begins before a claimant has reached the age of eighteen, however, an action may be brought at any time until the claimant's twentieth birthday.

UTAH [UTAH CODE ANN. § 78-14-4]

Action must be commenced within two years of the date when the injury was or should have been discovered, with a maximum limit of four years after the negligent act.

VERMONT [VT. STAT. ANN. TIT. 12, § 521]

Action must be commenced within three years from the date of the alleged malpractice or within two years from the date upon which the claimant knew or should have known of the alleged injury, whichever is later.

VIRGINIA [VA. CODE ANN. § 8.01-243]

Action must be commenced within two years from the date the cause of action accrued. An action by a minor must be commenced within two years from the date of the last act of negligence, unless the child is under eight years of age, in which case the action must be brought by the child's tenth birthday.

WASHINGTON [WASH. REV. CODE ANN. § 4.16.350; § 4.16.190]

Action must be commenced within three years of the act or omission alleged to have caused the injury or one year after the discovery of the alleged negligent act or omission, whichever period expires later. A claimant's minority, mental incompetence, or imprisonment tolls the limitations period.

WEST VIRGINIA [W. VA. CODE § 55-7B-4]

Action must be commenced within two years of either the date when the injury occurred or the date when the claimant discovered or reasonably should have discovered the injury, however no such action may be commenced more than ten years after the date of injury. A claimant under the age of ten must bring suit within two years of the date of the injury or prior to the claimant's twelfth birthday, whichever period is longer.

WISCONSIN [WIS. STAT. ANN. § 893.55(1)L § 893.55(3); § 893.56]

Action must be commenced within three years from the date of injury. Foreign object cases must be brought within one year from the date of discovery or three years from the date of the incident. Actions brought by or on behalf of a minor are subject to the above-noted limitation, or such actions must be brought by the time the minor reaches ten years of age, whichever is later.

WYOMING [WYO. STAT. ANN. § 1-3-107]

Action must be commenced within two years of discovery if the act, error, or omission was not reasonably discoverable within two years or was not discovered despite due diligence. If the claimant is a minor, he may also bring an action until his eighth birthday.

APPENDIX 8:
STATE CONTRIBUTORY AND
COMPARATIVE NEGLIGENCE RULES

JURISDICTION	APPLICABLE RULE
Alabama	Pure contributory negligence. A claimant's proximate contributory negligence will bar recovery completely.
Alaska	Pure comparative negligence. A claimant's fault does not bar recovery but his damages are reduced in proportion to the percentage of fault attributed to him.
Arizona	Pure comparative negligence. A claimant's fault does not bar recovery but his damages are reduced in proportion to the percentage of fault attributed to him.
Arkansas	Modified comparative negligence. A claimant's negligence diminishes his recovery by his percentage of fault but does not bar recovery unless the claimant's fault equals or exceeds the combined fault of the defendants. Otherwise, the claimant's recovery is diminished in proportion to his degree of negligence.
California	Pure comparative negligence. A claimant's fault does not bar recovery but his damages are reduced in proportion to the percentage of fault attributed to him.
Colorado	Modified comparative negligence. A claimant's contributory negligence will not bar recovery if the claimant's negligence was less than the defendant's negligence. Otherwise, the claimant's recovery is diminished in proportion to his degree of negligence.
Connecticut	Modified comparative negligence. A claimant's action is barred if his negligence exceeds the combined negligence of all defendants. Otherwise, the claimant's recovery is diminished in proportion to his degree of negligence.

JURISDICTION	APPLICABLE RULE
Delaware	Modified comparative negligence. A claimant's action is barred if his negligence exceeds the combined negligence of all defendants. Otherwise, the claimant's recovery is diminished in proportion to his degree of negligence.
District of Columbia	Pure contributory negligence. A claimant's proximate contributory negligence will bar recovery completely.
Florida	Pure comparative negligence. A claimant's award is diminished in proportion to the claimant's fault but the claimant's fault no matter how great, will not act as a bar to recovery.
Georgia	Variation of comparative negligence. A claimant's action is barred if he could have avoided the consequences of the defendant's negligence. Otherwise, the claimant's recovery is diminished in proportion to his degree of negligence.
Hawaii	Modified comparative negligence. A claimant's action is barred if his negligence exceeds the combined negligence of all defendants. Otherwise, the claimant's recovery is diminished in proportion to his degree of negligence.
Idaho	Individual rule form of contributory negligence. A claimant's contributory negligence does not bar recovery if the claimant's fault is less than the defendant's fault. The claimant is barred from recovery as to those defendants who are less negligent than he is.
Illinois	Modified comparative negligence. A claimant's action is barred if his negligence is more than 50 percent of the proximate cause of the injury or damage for which recovery is sought. Otherwise, the claimant's recovery is diminished in proportion to his percentage of fault.
Indiana	In cases brought under the Medical Malpractice Act, contributory negligence is held to be a complete defense that bars any recovery by plaintiff. In other cases, the Comparative Fault Act provides for a modified form of comparative negligence. Recovery is barred if the claimant's fault exceeds 50 percent of the total fault.
Iowa	Modified comparative negligence. A claimant's action is barred if his negligence exceeds the combined negligence of all other parties. Otherwise, the claimant's recovery is diminished in proportion to his degree of negligence.
Kansas	Modified comparative negligence. A claimant's action is barred if his negligence is equal to or greater than the combined negligence of all defendants. Otherwise, the claimant's recovery is diminished in proportion to his degree of negligence.

JURISDICTION	APPLICABLE RULE
Kentucky	Pure comparative negligence. A claimant's negligence does not bar recovery but any damage award must be reduced by the claimant's percentage of fault.
Louisiana	Pure comparative negligence in all cases except those of intentional tort. A claimant's recovery is reduced by his percentage of fault. In order to determine his percentage of fault, the fault of all other persons who contributed to the injury is considered whether or not they are parties.
Maine	Modified comparative negligence. A claimant's action is barred if the jury finds him to be equally at fault. Jury must reduce damages by an amount that it deems just and equitable and does not have to be in proportion to fault.
Maryland	Pure contributory negligence. A claimant's negligence will bar his recovery completely.
Massachusetts	Modified comparative negligence. A claimant's action is barred if his negligence exceeds the combined negligence of all defendants. Otherwise, the claimant's recovery is diminished in proportion to his degree of negligence.
Michigan	Pure comparative negligence with exception. A claimant's negligence does not bar recovery but causes damages to be reduced by the claimant's percentage of fault.
Minnesota	Modified comparative negligence. A claimant's action is barred if his fault exceeds the combined fault of all defendants. Otherwise, the claimant's recovery is diminished in proportion to his degree of fault. The negligence of non-parties is taken into account in apportioning fault.
Mississippi	Pure comparative negligence state. Miss. A claimant's damages are reduced by the amount of his negligence but recovery is not barred.
Missouri	Pure comparative negligence. A claimant's contributory fault does not bar recovery but diminishes the amount recoverable as compensatory damages in proportion to the claimant's degree of fault.
Montana	Modified comparative negligence. A claimant's action is barred if his negligence exceeds the combined negligence of all defendants and other persons. Otherwise, the claimant's recovery is diminished in proportion to his degree of negligence.
Nebraska	Comparative negligence. A claimant's negligence bars recovery only if it is equal to or greater than the total negligence of all defendants. Otherwise, the claimant's damages are reduced in proportion to his share of negligence.

JURISDICTION	APPLICABLE RULE
Nevada	Modified comparative negligence. A claimant's action is barred if his negligence exceeds the combined negligence of all defendants. Otherwise, the claimant's recovery is diminished in proportion to his degree of negligence.
New Hampshire	Modified comparative negligence. A claimant's action is barred only if his fault exceeds the combined fault of all defendants. The claimant's recovery is diminished in proportion to his degree of fault.
New Jersey	Modified comparative negligence. A claimant's action is barred if his negligence exceeds the combined negligence of all defendants. Otherwise, the claimant's recovery is diminished in proportion to his percentage of negligence
New Mexico	Pure form of comparative negligence. A claimant's negligence will never bar recovery but will only reduce the claimant's recovery in proportion to his fault.
New York	Pure comparative negligence. A claimant's negligence, no matter how great, will not bar recovery but the damages recoverable will be reduced in proportion to his negligence.
North Carolina	Pure contributory negligence. A claimant's contributory negligence bars recovery completely.
North Dakota	Modified comparative negligence. A claimant's action is barred if his fault equals or exceeds the combined fault of all others who contributed to the injury. Otherwise, the claimant's recovery is diminished in proportion to his degree of fault.
Ohio	Modified comparative negligence. A claimant's contributory negligence will' bar recovery if the claimant's negligence is greater than the combined negligence of all other persons whether or not such other persons are defendants or have already settled. Otherwise, a claimant's recoverable damages must be reduced in proportion to his percentage of negligence.
Oklahoma	Modified comparative negligence. A claimant's action is not barred unless his negligence exceeds the combined negligence of all defendants but his recovery is diminished in proportion to his negligence.
Oregon	Modified comparative negligence. A claimant's action is barred if his fault exceeds the combined fault of all defendants and persons who have settled. Otherwise, the claimant's recovery is diminished in proportion to his percentage of fault.

JURISDICTION	APPLICABLE RULE
Pennsylvania	Modified comparative negligence. A claimant is barred from recovery only if his contributory negligence was greater than the causal negligence of the defendants against whom recovery is sought. Otherwise, the claimant's damages are diminished in proportion to the amount of negligence attributed to the claimant
Rhode Island	Pure form of comparative negligence. A claimant's award is diminished in proportion to the claimant's negligence but the claimant's negligence, no matter how great, will not act as a bar to recovery.
South Carolina	Modified doctrine of comparative negligence. A claimant may recover damages if his negligence is less than or equal to that of all the defendants but his recovery shall be reduced in proportion to the amount of his negligence.
South Dakota	Modified form of comparative negligence. A claimant's contributory negligence does not bar recovery if the contributory negligence of the claimant was slight in comparison to the negligence of the defendant.
Tennessee	Modified comparative fault. A claimant may recover only if his negligence is less than the defendant's and his damages are reduced in proportion to the total negligence attributed to him.
Texas	Modified comparative negligence. A claimant's action is barred if his percentage of responsibility is greater than 50 percent. If his percentage of responsibility is 50 percent or less, the claimant's recovery is diminished in proportion to this percentage.
Utah	Modified comparative negligence. A claimant's action is barred only if his fault equals or exceeds the combined fault of all defendants and all persons immune from suit but the claimant's recovery is reduced in proportion to his degree of fault.
Vermont	Modified comparative negligence. A claimant's action is barred if his negligence is greater than the combined negligence of all defendants. Otherwise, the claimant's recovery is diminished in proportion to his degree of negligence.
Virginia	Pure contributory negligence whereby the negligence of the claimant bars recovery.
Washington	Pure comparative negligence. A claimant's award is diminished in proportion to the claimant's fault but the claimant's fault, no matter how great, will not act as a complete bar to recovery.

JURISDICTION   APPLICABLE RULE

West Virginia   Modified comparative negligence. A claimant's action is barred if his negligence equals or exceeds the combined negligence of all the other parties to the occurrence. Otherwise, the claimant's recovery is diminished in proportion to his degree of negligence

Wisconsin   Comparative negligence. A claimant's negligence does not bar recovery if that negligence was not greater than that of the person against whom recovery is sought. The claimant's negligence is compared separately to the negligence of each person against whom recovery is sought and damages are diminished in proportion to the claimant's negligence.

Wyoming   Modified comparative negligence. A claimant's contributory negligence will bar recovery if the claimant's negligence is more than 50 percent of the total fault. If the claimant's negligence is 50 percent or less of the total fault, the claimant's recovery is reduced in proportion to his percentage of fault.

APPENDIX 9:
STATE STATUTES GOVERNING JOINT AND SEVERAL LIABILITY IN MEDICAL MALPRACTICE CASES

JURISDICTION	STATUTE	APPLICABLE PROVISION
Alabama	None	None
Alaska	Alaska Statutes, § 09.17.080(d)	Multiple defendants liable only for their percentage of fault.
Arizona	Arizona Revised Statutes, § 12-2506	Multiple defendants liable only for their proportion of fault unless acting in concert or in an agency relationship.
Arkansas	Ark. Code Ann. § 16-61-203	A claimant may execute a judgment against any one of several joint tortfeasors regardless of the defendants' relative degrees of fault.
California	California Civil Procedure Code, § 1431.2	The liability of multiple defendants for noneconomic damages shall be in direct proportion to each defendant's proportion of fault.
Colorado	Colorado Revised Statutes, § 13-21-111.5	Procedures in section 13-20-602 which require plaintiff to file a certificate of review within 60 days after service of complaint shall apply if negligence or fault of nonparty is considered and nonparty is a licensed health care professional.

JURISDICTION	STATUTE	APPLICABLE PROVISION
Connecticut	Connecticut General Statutes Annotated, § 52-572a	Multiple defendants liable only for their proportionate share of fault unless award from any one defendant is uncollectible. In the event that recovery from one or more defendants is unrecoverable, the court will assess remaining defendants for a proportionate share of the uncollectible amount for noneconomic and economic damages.
Delaware	None	None
District of Columbia	None	None
Florida	Florida Statutes Annotated, § 768.81	Where damage award exceeds $258 000 the court will order multiple defendants to pay according to their respective proportion of fault, provided that with respect to any party whose fault equals or exceeds that of a particular plaintiff, court shall enter judgment on basis of doctrine of joint and several liability.
Georgia	Georgia Code, § 51-12-32, 33	Where the plaintiff is to some degree responsible for the injury, the jury may apportion the award of damages among the persons liable for the injury whose fault is greater than the plaintiff's. Where the jury so apportions liability for purposes of calculating damage payments, other defendants in the suit may not treat the liability as a joint one. Except where prohibited, contribution may be enforced among joint tortfeasors.
Hawaii	Haw. Rev. Stat. § 663-10.9	Liability for economic loss for personal injury and death is joint and several. Liability for non-economic damages is also joint and several if the tortfeasor is 25 percent negligent or more. That leaves as several only the liability of minor tortfeasors for non-economic damages.

JURISDICTION	STATUTE	APPLICABLE PROVISION
Idaho	Idaho Code, § 6-803	Where multiple defendants act in concert, or one defendant is the agent of another, there is a right of contribution between joint tortfeasors.
Illinois	735 ILCS 5/2-1117, 1118	Defendants are joint and severally liable only if defendant's negligence exceeds 25% of total fault attributable to plaintiff.
Indiana	Ind. Code Ann. § 34-51-2-8	In cases covered by the Comparative Fault Act, the trier of fact allocates liability on the basis of individual fault and a several judgment is granted against each defendant.
Iowa	Code of Iowa, § 668.4	Defendants whose liability is less than 50% of the total fault assigned to all parties are liable only for their proportion of fault.
Kansas	None	None
Kentucky	Kentucky Revised Statutes, § 411.182	Defendants are liable only for their proportion of fault.
Louisiana	La. Civ. Code Ann. art. 2324	A joint tortfeasor is not liable for more than his degree of fault and is not jointly liable with any other person for damages attributable to the fault of such person.
Maine	Me. Rev. Stat. Ann. tit. 14, § 156	Joint tortfeasors are jointly and severally liable thus any tortfeasor against whom judgment has been entered may be liable to the claimant for the entire judgment regardless of the tortfeasor's share of fault.
Maryland	None	Joint tortfeasors are jointly and severally liable thus each must assume and bear the responsibility for the misconduct of all.
Massachusetts	None	Joint tortfeasors are jointly and severally liable.

JURISDICTION	STATUTE	APPLICABLE PROVISION
Michigan	Michigan Comp. Laws, § 600.6304	Defendants shall be required to pay damages equal to their respective portions of fault. If part or all of defendant's liability is uncollectible, this portion of the judgment will be reallocated among remaining defendants according to their respective portions of fault in the case.
Minnesota	Minnesota Statutes, § 604.02	A person whose fault ins 15% or less may be jointly liable for a percentage of the whole award no greater than four times his percentage of fault.
Mississippi	Mississippi Code Annotated, § 85-5-7	Multiple defendants shall be liable in proportion to their fault, except that liability of multiple defendants shall be joint to the extent necessary for the plaintiff to recover 50% of his damages. Multiple defendants will also be jointly liable if they act in concert. In assessing percentages of fault, an employer and employee shall be considered as one defendant where employer's liability rests upon employee's negligence.
Missouri	Missouri Revised Statutes, § 538.230	Multiple defendants shall be jointly liable only with those defendants whose apportioned percentage of fault is equal to or less than such defendant.
Montana	Montana Code Annotated, § 27-1-703	Any party whose fault is 50% or less of the combined negligence of all parties is liable only for his hare of the fault. The remaining parties are jointly and severally liable. Parties are jointly liable if they act in concert or as an agent of another.
Nebraska	Revised Statutes of Nebraska, § 44-218 1858 10	Economic and non-economic damages shall be joint and several in cases involving two or more defendants acting in concert. In other actions involving more than one defendant, liability for economic damages shall be joint and several and liability for noneconomic damages shall be several only.

JURISDICTION	STATUTE	APPLICABLE PROVISION
Nevada	Nevada Revised Statutes, § 41.141	Where there are multiple defendants in a negligence action, each defendant is severally liable only for those damages equal to the proportion of fault attributable to each defendant, unless defendants have acted in concert. Concerted acts of the defendant does not include negligent acts committed by providers of health care while working together to provide treatment.<C5,5,0,0,0
New Hampshire	New Hampshire Revised Statutes Annotated, § 507:7e	If any party shall be less than 50% at fault, then that party's liability shall be several and shall be proportionate to their individual fault, except where parties acting in concert.
New Jersey	New Jersey Revised Statutes, § 2A:15-5.3	Parties who are 60% or more responsible for total damages are jointly and severally liable; parties who are at least 20% but less than 60% responsible are liable jointly and severally for the full amount of economic damages plus their proportion of fault for non-economic damages; parties liable for 20% or less of total damages are liable only for their proportion of fault.
New Mexico	New Mexico Statutes Annotated, § 41-3A-1	In any cause of action where comparative negligence applies, liability of joint tortfeasors shall be several and determined according to each defendant's proportion of fault. Joint and several liability applies only to a defendant acting intentionally, to defendants in an agency relationship, in a product liability action, or where public policy is served by application of the rule.
New York	New York Civil Practice Laws and Rules, § 1600-1602	Joint tortfeasors are jointly and severally liable, however, any joint tortfeasor whose liability is 50 percent or less of the tortfeasors' combined fault is severally liable only for the claimant's non-economic losses. Non- parties are not counted in this calculation if they could not be joined or are immune from liability.

JURISDICTION	STATUTE	APPLICABLE PROVISION
North Carolina	N.C. Gen. Stat. § 1B-1	Joint and several liability on joint tortfeasors thus any joint tortfeasor against whom judgment is entered is liable to the claimant for the entire amount of the judgment regardless of the tortfeasor's share of fault.
North Dakota	North Dakota Cent. Code, § 32-03.2-02	Only multiple defendants found to have acted in concert or encouraged or adopted tortious act for their benefit are jointly liable for all damages attributable to their combined percentage of fault. All others severally liable.
Ohio	Ohio Revised Code Annotated, § 2315.19	Each party jointly and severally liable for economic damages for noneconomic damages, where plaintiff contributorily negligent, each defendant is liable only for his proportionate share of fault.
Oklahoma	None	Joint tortfeasors are jointly and severally liable when the recovering claimant is without fault.
Oregon	Oregon Revised Statutes, § 18.485	The liability of each defendant in a personal injury action for noneconomic damages shall be several only. The liability of a defendant who is less than 15% at fault for economic damages shall be several only. The liability of a defendant who is at least 15% at fault for the economic damages shall be joint and several, except that a defendant whom percentage of fault is less than that allocated to the plaintiff is liable to the plaintiff only for that percentage of the recoverable economic damages.
Pennsylvania	42 Pa. Cons. Stat. Ann. § 7102	Liability is joint and several thus a claimant may recover the full amount of the allowed recovery from any joint tortfeasor against whom recovery is not barred.
Rhode Island	Rhode Island General Laws, § 10-6-2	Two or more persons jointly or severally liable in tort for the same injury. Applicable to physicians.

JURISDICTION	STATUTE	APPLICABLE PROVISION
South Carolina	South Carolina Code Annotated, § 15-38-10	Joint tortfeasors severally liable only according to their proportionate fault.
South Dakota	South Dakota Codified Laws Annotated, § 15-8-15.1	Any defendant allocated less than 50% of the total fault allocated to all the parties may not be jointly liable for more than twice the percentage of fault allocated to that party.
Tennessee	Tenn. Code Ann. §§ 29-11-101 to 106	With the adoption of comparative fault in place of contributory negligence, the doctrine of joint and several liability became obsolete and although statute remains on the books, case law holds that its provisions no longer determine the apportionment of liability between co-defendants, and that each tortfeasor is now liable only for the percentage of plaintiff's damages occasioned by his own negligence.
Texas	Texas Civil Practice Code Annotated, § 33.013	Defendants are jointly and severally liable only where the percentage of responsibility is greater than 20% and is greater than the plaintiff's responsibility, or where the defendant's responsibility is greater than 10% and the plaintiff has no responsibility.
Utah	Utah Code Annotated, § 78-27-40	Defendant severally liable only in proportion to amount of fault attributed to that defendant.
Vermont	Vt. Stat. Ann. tit. 12 § 1036	Joint tortfeasors are not jointly and severally liable but are only severally liable thus a joint tortfeasor is liable only for that portion of a judgment which is equal to the proportion the tortfeasor's fault bears to the joint tortfeasors' combined fault.
Virginia	Va. Code Ann. § 8.01-443	Joint tortfeasors are joint and severally liable thus any joint tortfeasor against whom a judgment is entered is liable to the claimant for the entire judgment regardless of the tortfeasor's share of fault.

JURISDICTION	STATUTE	APPLICABLE PROVISION
Washington	Washington Revised Code Annotated, § 4.22.070	Liability of each defendant shall be joint only if parties acted in concert or their was an agency relationship, or if the jury determines that the plaintiff was not at fault, the defendants shall be jointly and severally liable for the sum of their proportionate shares of plaintiff's total damages.
West Virginia	West Virginia Code, § 55-7B-9	Defendants in medical injury suits bearing more than 25% of the liability shall be jointly and severally liable.
Wisconsin	Wis. Stat. Ann. § 895.045	Under the statutory system of comparative negligence only a defendant found to be 51 percent or more causally negligent is jointly and severally liable. A defendant who is less than 51 percent causally negligent is liable only for his own percentage of negligence unless he acted as part of a common scheme or plan.
Wyoming	Wyo. Stat. Ann. § 1-1-109(d)	Allocated several liability thus a defendant is liable only for that portion of the total damages that is equal to his percentage of fault

APPENDIX 10:
STATE STATUTES GOVERNING LIMITS ON DAMAGE AWARDS IN MEDICAL MALPRACTICE CASES

JURISDICTION	STATUTE	APPLICABLE PROVISION
Alabama	Alabama Code, § 6-5-544; 547	$400,000 limit on non-economic damages including punitive damages; $1 million limit on wrongful death actions.
Alaska	Alaska Statutes, § 09.17.010	Noneconomic losses may not exceed $500,000 but this limit does not apply to damages for disfigurement or severe physical impairment.
Arizona	Arizona State Constitution, Article 2, § 31	No law shall be enacted limiting damages for death or injury.
Arkansas	None	There is no Arkansas statutory provision which limits attorney's fees in a medical malpractice action.
California	California Civil Procedure Code, § 3333.2	The amount of noneconomic damages may not exceed $250,000.
Colorado	Colorado Revised Statutes, § 13-64-302	Damages for medical malpractice against a hospital or physician may not exceed $1,000,000 per patient, including any derivative claim by any other claimant. of that $1,000,000, not more than $250,000 may be attributable to non-economic loss or injury

JURISDICTION	STATUTE	APPLICABLE PROVISION
Connecticut	None	Connecticut does not impose a cap on damages recoverable in medical malpractice actions.
Delaware	None	Delaware does not place a limit on the damages a claimant may recover.
District of Columbia	None	The District of Columbia does not place a cap on the amount of damages recoverable in a medical malpractice action.
Florida	Florida Statutes Annotated, § 768.73	Florida's voluntary arbitration scheme provides a cap on non-economic damages under certain circumstances.
Georgia	Ga. Code Ann. § 51-12-5.1	Georgia does not place a cap on the amount of compensatory damages that may be awarded. Punitive damages are capped at $250,000 unless the claimant can successfully demonstrate that the defendant had an intent to harm.
Hawaii	Haw. Rev. Stat. § 663-8.7	Hawaii has a statute that imposes a $375,000 damage limit for the recovery of damages for pain and suffering.
Idaho	Idaho Code, § 6-1603	Noneconomic damages shall not exceed $400,000 unless personal injury caused by willful or reckless misconduct or circumstances that would constitute a felony. This cap shall increase or decrease yearly according to the state's adjustment of the average annual wage.
Illinois	735 Ill. Comp. Stat. Ann. § 5/2-1115.1	Illinois' $500,000 cap on non-economic damages in medical malpractice cases held to be unconstitutional.
Indiana	Ind. Code Ann. § 34-18-14-3	The limit for each qualified provider is $250,000 and the total cap on damages against all qualified providers and the Patient Compensation Fund is $1,250,000.
Iowa	None	Iowa does not place a cap on the amount of damages recoverable in a medical malpractice action.

JURISDICTION	STATUTE	APPLICABLE PROVISION
Kansas	Kan. Stat. Ann. § 60-3407	The statute's cap on damages in medical malpractice actions was held to create an unconstitutional limitation on the right to trial by jury.
Kentucky	None	Kentucky does not impose a statutory cap on damages recoverable in medical malpractice actions.
Louisiana	None	There is no damage cap applicable to those not insured by the state but qualified health care providers have their liability limited to $100,000.
Maine	Me. Rev. Stat. Ann. tit. 18-A, § 2-804	Maine does not impose a cap on the amount of damages that may be collected in a medical malpractice action. However, non- economic damages for wrongful death are limited to $150,000 and punitive damages are limited to $75,000.
Maryland	M Md. Code Ann., Cts. & Jud. Proc. § 11-108	Maryland imposes a limit on recoverable non-economic damages for any personal injury cause of action for medical malpractice accruing after July 1, 1986. The limit was originally $350,000 but for causes of actions arising on or after October 1, 1994, the limit has been increased to $500,000. As of October 1, 1995, and every October 1 thereafter, the limit on non-economic damages is increased by $15,000

JURISDICTION	STATUTE	APPLICABLE PROVISION
Massachusetts	Massachusetts General laws Annotated, Chapter 231, § 60H	The plaintiff shall be awarded no more than $500,000 for non-economic damages unless the jury determines that there is a substantial or permanent loss or impairment of bodily function or substantial disfigurement, or other special circumstances which warrant a finding that the cap was unfair. If the total amount of general damages from a single occurrence for all plaintiffs exceeds $500,000, then the amount of such damages recoverable by each plaintiff will be reduced to a percentage of $500,000 proportionate to that plaintiff's share of the total amount of such damages for all plaintiffs.
Michigan	Mich. Comp. Laws Ann. § 600.6304(5)	The maximum recoverable by all plaintiffs resulting from the negligence of all defendants is $280,000, adjusted annually for inflation, except in instances of paralysis due to brain or spinal cord injury, impairment of cognitive capacity, or loss of reproductive ability, in which case the limit is $500,000. Any jury award in excess of this amount will be reduced by the court.
Minnesota	None	Minnesota has not enacted a cap on the damages that can be awarded in a medical malpractice case.
Mississippi	None	Mississippi does not place a cap on the damages a claimant can collect in a medical malpractice case.
Missouri	Missouri Revised Statutes, § 538.210	No plaintiff in an action against health care provider shall recover more than $500,000 per occurrence for noneconomic damages from any one defendant. This limit shall be increased or decreased on an annual basis effective January 1st of each year in accordance with figures determined by the U.S. Department of Commerce.

JURISDICTION	STATUTE	APPLICABLE PROVISION
Montana	Mont. Code Ann. § 25-9-411	For medical malpractice causes of action there is a limit of $250,000 on the non-economic damages a claimant can recover.
Nebraska	None	Nebraska does not generally impose limits on the amount recoverable as compensatory damages in medical malpractice actions.
Nevada	None	Nevada does not set a cap on compensatory damages awarded in medical malpractice cases.
New Hampshire	N.H. Rev. Stat. Ann § 507-C:7	The New Hampshire Supreme Court has held $250,000 cap on non-economic damages in medical malpractice cases to be unconstitutional.
New Jersey	N.J. Stat. Ann. § 2A:15-5.14(b)	No defendant is liable for any punitive damages in any action for an amount in excess of five times the liability of that defendant for compensatory damages, or $350,000, whichever is greater.
New Mexico	New Mexico Statutes Annotated, § 41-5-6	Limit for aggregate dollar amount recoverable is $600,000.
New York	None	New York does not limit the amount of damages recoverable in medical malpractice actions.
North Carolina	N.C. Gen. Stat. § 1D-25	North Carolina generally does not limit the compensatory damages recoverable in medical malpractice actions. However, for actions filed on or after January 1, 1996, punitive damages will be limited to three times compensatory damages or $250,000 whichever is greater.
North Dakota	N.D. Cent. Code § 32-62-02 (1996)	There is a $500,000 cap on non-economic damages in medical malpractice cases.
Ohio	Ohio Rev. Code Ann. § 2323.54	Non-economic damages are limited to the greater of $250,000 or three times economic damages to a maximum of $500,000.

JURISDICTION	STATUTE	APPLICABLE PROVISION
Oklahoma	Okla. Stat. Ann. tit. 23, § 9.1	In cases of reckless disregard of the rights of others, punitive damages are limited to $100,000. In cases of intentional and malicious acts, they are limited to the greater of $500,000, twice compensatory damages, or the benefit derived by defendant from his conduct. If the judge finds beyond a reasonable doubt that the intentional and malicious act threatened human life, the cap does not apply.
Oregon	Or. Rev. Stat. § 18.560	Statute's $500,000 cap on damages for non-economic loss in bodily injury and death cases held to be unconstitutional under most circumstances.
Pennsylvania	40 Pa. Cons. Stat. Ann. § 1301.812-A(g)	Pennsylvania does not impose a cap on compensatory damages. Punitive damages against individual physicians shall not exceed 200 percent of compensatory damages but shall not be less than $100,000 unless a lower verdict for compensatory damages is returned by the trier of fact.
Rhode Island	R.I. Gen. Laws § 9-1-8; § 10-7-2	Punitive damages are not recoverable in any action brought by or against the executor or administrator of an estate. There is a $100,000 minimum recovery in any wrongful death action.
South Carolina	None	South Carolina does not impose a cap on the amount of damages that a claimant can recover in a medical malpractice case.
South Dakota	S.D. Codified Laws Ann. § 21-3-11	In any medical malpractice action in South Dakota the total general damages may not exceed $500,000.
Tennessee	None	Tennessee does not place a cap on the amount of damages recoverable in a medical malpractice action.

JURISDICTION	STATUTE	APPLICABLE PROVISION
Texas	Tex. Rev. Civ. Stat. Ann. art. 4590i, § 11.02	Texas law limits damages in a medical malpractice action for wrongful death to $500,000 as of 1997 adjusted annually for inflation
Utah	Utah Code Ann. § 78-14-7.1	In a medical malpractice action, non-economic damages (those for pain, suffering, and inconvenience) may not exceed $250,000.
Vermont	None	Vermont does not place a cap on the amount of damages a claimant may recover in a medical malpractice action.
Virginia	Va. Code Ann. § 8.01-581.15	Virginia imposes a $1,000,000 damage cap on recoveries for bodily injury or death in medical malpractice cases.

APPENDIX 11:
STATES RULES GOVERNING PATIENT COMPENSATION FUNDS OR STATE-SPONSORED LIABILITY INSURANCE FOR PHYSICIANS

ALABAMA

Alabama does not have a patient compensation fund or a program of state-sponsored liability insurance for physicians.

ALASKA

Alaska does not have a patient compensation fund or a program of state-sponsored liability insurance for physicians.

ARIZONA

Arizona does not have a patient compensation fund or a program of state-sponsored liability insurance for physicians.

ARKANSAS

Arkansas does not have a patient compensation fund or a program of state-sponsored liability insurance for physicians.

CALIFORNIA

California does not have a patient compensation fund or a program of state-sponsored liability insurance for physicians.

COLORADO [COLO. REV. STAT. ANN. § 13-64-301]

Physicians and hospitals must achieve and maintain statutory financial responsibility. A physician establishes financial responsibility by maintaining commercial professional liability insurance coverage in a minimum amount of $500,000 per incident and $1,500,000 in the annual aggregate, or by possessing equivalent security, such as a surety bond, cash deposited with the commissioner of insurance, or self-insurance. A hospital establishes its financial responsibility in the same manner except that a hospital's annual aggregate must be at least $3,000,000.

CONNECTICUT

Connecticut does not have a patient compensation fund or a program of state-sponsored liability insurance for physicians.

DELAWARE

Delaware does not have a patient compensation fund or a program of state-sponsored liability insurance for physicians.

DISTRICT OF COLUMBIA

The District of Columbia does not have a patient compensation fund or a program of state-sponsored liability insurance for physicians.

FLORIDA [FLA. STAT. ANN. § 766.303; FLA. STAT. ANN. § 766.105]

Florida has established two patient compensation funds: (a) The Florida Birth-Related Neurological Injury Compensation Plan; and (b) The Florida Patient Compensation Fund. The Florida Birth-Related Neurological Injury Compensation Act ("NICA") is the exclusive means of obtaining compensation for an important class of severe, birth-related injuries and provides compensation for birth-related neurological injuries without regard to the negligence of any health care provider. The Florida Patient Compensation Fund is a statutory system of state-sponsored excess insurance for medical malpractice liability under which hospitals are required to participate in the fund by paying a yearly fee and obtaining primary insurance of $250,000 per claim or $500,000 per occurrence, adjustable by inflation.

GEORGIA

Georgia does not have a patient compensation fund or a program of state-sponsored liability insurance for physicians.

HAWAII

Hawaii does not have a patient compensation fund or a program of state-sponsored liability insurance for physicians.

IDAHO

Idaho does not have a patient compensation fund or a program of state-sponsored liability insurance for physicians.

ILLINOIS

Illinois does not have a patient compensation fund or a program of state-sponsored liability insurance for physicians.

INDIANA [IND. CODE ANN. § 34-18-2-24.5; § 34-18-3-2]

The Indiana Medical Malpractice Act establishes a Patient Compensation Fund that functions as a system of excess insurance for health care providers. To become a "qualified provider," entitled to the benefits of the Act, a health care provider must file proof of financial responsibility and pay the surcharge assessed by the Commissioner of Insurance to support the Fund. A qualified provider establishes financial responsibility by purchasing malpractice liability insurance in the statutorily prescribed amount. The maximum liability of a qualified provider for an occurrence is limited to the amount of required insurance. The Patient Compensation Fund is liable for the excess over what is owed by all the qualified providers up to the statutory damage cap.

IOWA

Iowa does not have a patient compensation fund or a program of state-sponsored liability insurance for physicians.

KANSAS [KAN. STAT. ANN. § 40-3402; § 40-3403]

Kansas requires all health care providers to carry liability insurance in the statutorily prescribed amount and has established a Health Care Stabilization Fund, which provides coverage to health care providers in excess of their required primary limits.

KENTUCKY

Kentucky does not have a patient compensation fund or a program of state-sponsored liability insurance for physicians.

LOUISIANA [LA. REV. STAT. ANN. § 40:1299.44; § 40:1299.38]

The Louisiana Medical Malpractice Act established a Patient's Compensation Fund under which state health care providers are automatically entitled to be covered by the fund provided they file proof that they are covered by a policy of malpractice liability insurance in the statutorily prescribed amount per claim and pay the surcharge assessed by the Louisiana Insurance Rating Commission. Judgments, settlements, or binding arbitration orders in excess of the statutorily prescribed amount per provider are paid out of the fund.

MAINE

Maine does not have a patient compensation fund or a program of state-sponsored liability insurance for physicians.

MARYLAND

Maryland does not have a patient compensation fund or a program of state-sponsored liability insurance for physicians.

MASSACHUSETTS [MASS. ANN. LAWS CH. 112, § 2]

Massachusetts does not have a patient compensation fund or a program of state-sponsored liability insurance for physicians, however, the board of registration in medicine can promulgate rules requiring physicians to carry malpractice liability insurance in statutorily prescribed amounts. it prescribes.

MICHIGAN

Michigan does not have a patient compensation fund or a program of state-sponsored liability insurance for physicians.

MINNESOTA

Minnesota does not have a patient compensation fund or a program of state-sponsored liability insurance for physicians.

MISSISSIPPI [MISS. CODE ANN. § 41-13-11]

Mississippi does not have a patient compensation fund or a program of state-sponsored liability insurance for physicians, however, hospitals may participate in a joint trust fund agreement for the purpose of providing insurance against professional liability.

MISSOURI [MO. ANN. STAT. § 383.500]

Missouri does not have a patient compensation fund, however, any physician on the medical staff of a hospital located in a county with a population exceeding 75,000 must furnish evidence of medical malpractice insurance in a statutorily prescribed amount unless the physician's practice is limited exclusively to patients seen or treated at a hospital and the physician is insured exclusively under the hospital's policy of insurance or its self-insurance program.

MONTANA

Montana does not have a patient compensation fund or a program of state-sponsored liability insurance for physicians.

NEBRASKA [NEB. REV. STAT. § 44-2829; § 44-2824]

Nebraska provides an excess liability fund for the benefit of qualified health care providers who file proof of financial responsibility and pay a surcharge. Once a health care provider has qualified under the Act, the Act becomes the exclusive method of recovery, unless the claimant has elected in writing prior to treatment not to come under the provisions of the Act.

NEVADA

Nevada does not have a patient compensation fund or a program of state-sponsored liability insurance for physicians.

NEW HAMPSHIRE

New Hampshire does not have a patient compensation fund or a program of state-sponsored liability insurance for physicians.

NEW JERSEY

New Jersey does not have a patient compensation fund or a program of state-sponsored liability insurance for physicians.

NEW MEXICO [N.M. STAT. ANN. § 41-5-25; § 41-5-5; 6]

New Mexico has established a patient's compensation fund financed by a surcharge on all qualified health care providers. Health care providers must also carry liability insurance in a statutorily prescribed amount. The excess over the statutorily prescribed amount per occurrence of any judgment obtained in a medical malpractice action is paid by the patient's compensation fund, except for punitive damages.

NEW YORK

New York does not have a patient compensation fund or a program of state-sponsored liability insurance for physicians.

NORTH CAROLINA

North Carolina does not have a patient compensation fund or a program of state-sponsored liability insurance for physicians.

NORTH DAKOTA [N.D. CENT. CODE § 26.1-14-11]

North Dakota has established the North Dakota Medical Malpractice Mutual Insurance Company under which the liability of any policyholder carrying applicable insurance with limits in a statutorily prescribed amount may not exceed the amount of coverage.

OHIO

Ohio does not have a patient compensation fund or a program of state-sponsored liability insurance for physicians.

OKLAHOMA

Oklahoma does not have a patient compensation fund or a program of state-sponsored liability insurance for physicians.

OREGON

Oregon does not have a patient compensation fund or a program of state-sponsored liability insurance for physicians.

PENNSYLVANIA [40 PA. CONS. STAT. ANN. § 1301.701]

Pennsylvania has a Medical Professional Liability Catastrophe Loss Fund ("CAT Fund") that provides excess insurance to all health care providers in the state. Health care providers are required to obtain a prescribed amount of basic insurance coverage and are then entitled to and required to obtain excess coverage from the CAT Fund, paid for by an annual surcharge. After the exhaustion of the CAT Fund limit, the health care provider may be individually liable.

RHODE ISLAND

Rhode Island does not have a patient compensation fund or a program of state-sponsored liability insurance for physicians.

SOUTH CAROLINA [S.C. CODE ANN. § 38-79-420; § 38-79-440]

South Carolina has established a Patients' Compensation Fund which is responsible for the payment of that portion of any medical malpractice or general liability judgment or settlement which exceeds a statutorily prescribed amount. All health care providers have the option of participating in the Fund and must pay an annual fee.

SOUTH DAKOTA

South Dakota does not have a patient compensation fund or a program of state-sponsored liability insurance for physicians.

TENNESSEE

Tennessee does not have a patient compensation fund or a program of state-sponsored liability insurance for physicians.

TEXAS

Texas does not have a patient compensation fund or a program of state-sponsored liability insurance for physicians.

UTAH

Utah does not have a patient compensation fund or a program of state-sponsored liability insurance for physicians.

VERMONT

Vermont does not have a patient compensation fund or a program of state-sponsored liability insurance for physicians.

VIRGINIA [VA. CODE ANN. § 38.2-5000 - § 38.2- 5021]

Virginia does not have a general patient compensation fund covering all medical malpractice claims but has enacted the Birth-Related Neurological Injury Compensation Act which provides the exclusive right of recovery for permanently disabled infants suffering from a birth-related neurological injury. To qualify for assistance, the claimant's physician and delivery hospital must participate in the program by paying an assessment.

WASHINGTON

Washington does not have a patient compensation fund or a program of state-sponsored liability insurance for physicians.

WEST VIRGINIA

West Virginia does not have a patient compensation fund or a program of state-sponsored liability insurance for physicians.

WISCONSIN [WIS. STAT. ANN. § 655.23; § 655.27]

Wisconsin has established the Wisconsin Patients Compensation Fund under which health care providers must pay a yearly assessment into the fund and provide proof of financial responsibility to the Commissioner of Insurance in a statutorily prescribed amount. The Fund provides compensation for claimants whose damages exceed the health care provider's liability insurance.

WYOMING [WYO. STAT. ANN. § 26-33-101 - § 26-33-105]

The Wyoming legislature has created a medical liability compensation fund to provide physicians with excess insurance coverage whereby a physician must obtain malpractice insurance in a statutorily prescribed amount and the fund pays any medical malpractice judgment or settlement in excess of the amount of insurance up to a statutorily prescribed amount per year per physician.

APPENDIX 12:
STATE COLLATERAL SOURCE RULES IN MEDICAL MALPRACTICE CASES

JURISDICTION	STATUTE	APPLICABLE PROVISION
Alabama	Code of Alabama, § 6-5-545	Discretionary offset; evidence of payment or future payment for medical expenses incurred by plaintiff and evidence of costs of obtaining such reimbursement or repayment is admissible.
Alaska	Alaska Statutes, § 09.55.548(b)	Mandatory offset; plaintiff may only receive damages from defendant which exceed amounts compensated by collateral sources except federal program sources which by law seek subrogation and death benefits from life insurance.
Arizona	Arizona Revised Statutes, § 12-565	Discretionary offset; defendant may introduce evidence of collateral source of payment for economic losses. Plaintiff may introduce evidence of payment made to obtain collateral source or that recovery from defendant subject to lien or statutory subrogation.
Arkansas	None	A claimant's receipt of compensation from collateral sources does not reduce the claimant's recoverable damages.

JURISDICTION	STATUTE	APPLICABLE PROVISION
California	California Civil Procedure Code, § 3333.1	Discretionary offset; defendant may introduce evidence of collateral sources; plaintiff may introduce evidence of payments made to secure collateral source benefits. No source of collateral benefits introduced pursuant to this provision shall recovery any amount from plaintiff or be subrogated to plaintiff's rights. No collateral source shall obtain reimbursement from a medical malpractice defendant.
Colorado	Colorado Revised Statutes, § 13-21-111.6	Mandatory offset; the court will reduce amount of verdict by the sum of collateral source compensation except if the plaintiff purchased insurance that is the collateral source.
Connecticut	Connecticut General Statutes Annotated, § 52-225a	Mandatory offset; the court shall reduce the award of economic damages by the amount of compensation received from collateral sources except where a right of subrogation exists. Plaintiff may submit evidence of payments made for collateral source benefits.
Delaware	Delaware Code Annotated, Title 18, § 6862	Discretionary offset; evidence of public collateral source of compensation may be introduced including any prospective changes in the marital, financial, or other status of any person benefiting from payment of damages; no evidence of life insurance proceeds or other private collateral sources of compensation.
District of Columbia	None	Claimant's receipt of payments from collateral sources will not serve to reduce the claimant's damages.
Florida	Florida Statutes Annotated, § 768.76	Mandatory offset of damages where liability is admitted or found by trial court by the total of all collateral source payment with exception of those collateral sources for which there are subrogation rights. Reduction shall be offset by amount paid by plaintiff, on behalf of plaintiff, or by immediate family, to obtain collateral source benefits.

JURISDICTION	STATUTE	APPLICABLE PROVISION
Georgia	Georgia Code, § 51-12-1	Discretionary offset; evidence of compensation from all collateral sources and costs thereof admissible for consideration by trier of fact.
Hawaii	None	Payments to the claimant from collateral sources are not considered in calculating the claimant's damages.
Idaho	Idaho Code, § 6-1606	Mandatory offset of collateral sources except federal benefits, life insurance, and subrogation rights.
Illinois	735 ILCS 5/2-1205	Mandatory offset; award to plaintiff shall be reduced by an amount equal to the sum of 50% of lost income collateral source benefits and 100% of health insurance benefits, except if such medial or hospital expenses are directly attributable to the medical injury at issue and to the extent there are subrogation rights. The offset shall not exceed more than 50% of the award and the offset may be reduced by the amount paid by plaintiff when the preceding two years to obtain such collateral source benefits.
Indiana	Indiana Code Annotated, § 34-44-1-2	In personal injury or wrongful death cases, proof is admissible of all collateral source payments except the following: (a) payments of life insurance or other death benefits, (b) insurance benefits for which the claimant or his family paid directly, and (c) payments made by Indiana or the United States prior to trial to compensate the claimant for his loss.—The claimant may introduce evidence of any repayment of collateral source benefits he is required to make, and the claimant may offer proof of the cost to the claimant or his family of collateral benefits.
Iowa	Code of Iowa, § 147.136	Economic damages in a medical malpractice case may not include amounts that have been or will be replaced or indemnified by insurance, or by governmental, employment, or service benefit programs, or from any other source except the assets of the claimant or of the members of the claimant's immediate family.

JURISDICTION	STATUTE	APPLICABLE PROVISION
Kansas	Kansas Statutes, § 60-3801	In any action for personal injury or death alleging damages in excess of $150,000, evidence of collateral sources is admissible and shall be used to reduce any damage award. Note: Kansas statute permitting collateral benefits to be deducted from a judgment has been held unconstitutional.
Kentucky	Kentucky Revised Statutes, § 411.188(3)	Discretionary offset; evidence of collateral source benefits, except life insurance, shall be admissible as well as the value of plaintiff premiums paid by or on behalf of plaintiff to obtain benefits and any subrogation rights.
Louisiana	None	A tortfeasor may not benefit, and an injured plaintiff's recovery may not be diminished, because of benefits received by the plaintiff from other sources.
Maine	Maine Revised Statutes Annotated, Title 24, § 2906	Mandatory offset; the court shall reduce the amount of the economic damage award by the amount of all collateral sources of benefits that have not exercised subrogation rights within 10 days after verdict for the plaintiff. The offset may be reduced by amounts paid by the plaintiff to obtain collateral benefits in the two year period immediately preceding the injury and the portion of plaintiff's total costs to prosecute the action, including attorney fees, may be reduced by an amount equal to the percentage that the offset is of the total award.
Maryland	None	Evidence of the claimant's receipt of payments from collateral sources may not be admitted to reduce his damages.
Massachusetts	Massachusetts General Laws Annotated, Chapter 231, § 60G	In medical malpractice jury action, the deduction of collateral benefits is performed by the judge after the verdict. Most collateral sources are covered except benefits provided under federal laws providing for a right of subrogation against the recovery.

JURISDICTION	STATUTE	APPLICABLE PROVISION
Michigan	Michigan Comp. Laws, § 600.6303	Mandatory offset; evidence that economic damages sought h ave been or will be paid by collateral source, except life insurance benefits or lien holder, is admissible after verdict for the plaintiff. The amount of the offset will be reduced by the amount of premiums paid by plaintiff his family, or his employer.
Minnesota	Minnesota Statutes, § 548.36	Mandatory offset; the court shall reduce the award by the amounts of collateral source benefits, except those with subrogation rights or contributed by plaintiff or his family for two years preceding action, and shall reduce the amount of offset by the amount paid by plaintiff or his family to obtain benefits.
Mississippi	None	Defendants in medical malpractice actions may not make reference to any forms of collateral payments to the claimant for the alleged injury and c ollateral source payments may not be credited or used to reduce the claimant's damages.
Missouri	None	A defendant is not entitled to a reduction in the claimant's damages by proving the claimant has received or will receive compensation for the loss from a source independent of the defendant.
Montana	Montana Code Annotated, § 27-1-308	Mandatory offset; where total award exceeds $50,000 and plaintiff will receive full award, the court must reduce the award by the amount of collateral source benefits that do not have subrogation rights. Amounts that a plaintiff has p aid for the previous five years, or will pay, for life insurance benefits, must be deducted from the offset.
Nebraska	Revised Statutes of Nebraska, § 44-2819	Discretionary offset; evidence of nonrefundable collateral source benefits may be taken as credit, less premium payments, against the judgment, but such evidence shall not be introduced to the jury.

JURISDICTION	STATUTE	APPLICABLE PROVISION
Nevada	Nevada Revised Statutes, § 42.020	Damages must be reduced by amount of any prior payment made by the health care provider to the injured person or claimant to meet reasonable expenses and other essential goods and services or reasonable living expenses.
New Hampshire	New Hampshire Revised Statutes Annotated, § 507-C:7	Statute abolishing the collateral source rule in medical malpractice actions held unconstitutional.
New Jersey	New Jersey Revised Statutes, § 2A:15-97	Mandatory offset; collateral source benefits not including worker's compensation or life insurance benefits, shall be admissible and deducted from award, less any premium paid by plaintiff or plaintiff's family.
New Mexico	None	Evidence of a claimant's receipt of payments from collateral sources is inadmissible.
New York	New York Civil Practice Laws and Rules, § 4545	Mandatory offset; the court shall reduce the economic award by the amount of any collateral source benefit, except those sources with liens against the plaintiff. The court shall reduce the offset by the amount of premiums paid by plaintiff for such benefits for the two-year period immediately preceding and less the amount equal to the projected future cost of maintaining the benefit.
North Carolina	None	The deduction of collateral benefits from a claimant's damages is prohibited.
North Dakota	North Dakota Cent. Code, § 32-03.2-06	Mandatory offset; economic damages will be reduced by the amount of collateral source benefits not subject to any subrogation rights against plaintiff, or collateral source benefits purchased by the plaintiff, or life insurance benefits.
Ohio	Ohio Revised Code Annotated, § 2317.45	The trier of fact shall consider evidence of collateral benefits that have been paid or will be paid. The definition of collateral source excludes life insurance and insurance for which plaintiff paid a premium, but includes workers' compensation.

JURISDICTION	STATUTE	APPLICABLE PROVISION
Oklahoma	None	Payments received by a claimant from collateral sources may be deducted from the claimant's damages.
Oregon	Oregon Revised Statutes, § 18.580	Discretionary offset; court may deduct from the award the total amount of collateral source benefits other than benefits plaintiff must repay, life insurance, other insurance benefits for w which plaintiff or his family paid premiums, retirement, disability and pension plan benefits, including federal social security benefits.
Pennsylvania	None	a medical malpractice claimant is entitled to the damages caused by the defendant's negligence regardless of the compensation the claimant receives from other sources.
Rhode Island	Rhode Island General Laws, § 9-19-34.1	The plaintiff's award shall be reduced by jury or court by the amount of collateral benefits received less the amount paid to secure such benefits. The lien of a first party payor who has paid such a benefit shall be foreclosed.
South Carolina	None	Medical malpractice defendants may not offer evidence of the claimant's receipt of payments from third parties, such as insurance, as a means of reducing the claimant's recovery.
South Dakota	South Dakota Codified Laws Annotated, § 21-3-12	Discretionary offset; Where special damages are alleged, such damages may be reduced by the amount of collateral source benefits covering such damages, except to the extent that such benefits have a right of subrogation, purchased by plaintiff or his family, or are payable by government programs not subject to subrogation.
Tennessee	Tennessee Code Annotated, § 29-26-119	Mandatory offset; economic damages must be reduced by the amount of collateral source benefits received, except for assets contributed by plaintiff or his family and insurance purchased privately and individually.

JURISDICTION	STATUTE	APPLICABLE PROVISION
Texas	None	A claimant's receipt of benefits from a collateral sourcesuch as insurancedoes not reduce his recovery.
Utah	Utah Code Annotated, § 78-14-4.5	Mandatory offset; the court shall reduce the award by the total of all amounts from collateral source benefits, except those benefits for which subrogation rights exist. The court shall reduce offset by amounts paid by or on behalf of plaintiff to obtain benefits.
Vermont	None	Payments received by the claimant from collateral sources may not be offered as evidence to reduce the claimant's recoverable damages.
Virginia	None	A claimant's receipt of collateral payments does not reduce his recovery.
Washington	Washington Revised Code Annotated, § 7.70.080	Discretionary offset; evidence that the plaintiff has been compensated for injury from any sources, except patient or family assets, or insurance purchased by plaintiff or his employer, is admissible.
West Virginia	None	Damages are not reduced by collateral benefits the claimant has received as compensation for injuries for which he has recovered.
Wisconsin	Wis. Stat. Ann. § 893.55(7)	Evidence of any compensation from a collateral source is admissible in an action to recover damages for medical malpractice.
Wyoming	None	A claimant's receipt of collateral benefits does not serve to reduce his recovery.

APPENDIX 13:
COMMONLY USED MEDICAL TERMS

Active Motion: A voluntary movement made by a person, or the extent to which he will move a member of his body.

Adhesion: The uniting of one surface with another by scar tissue.

Aneurysm: A dilation, or saccule formation, of an artery. The source may be congenital, luetic, or arteriosclerotic.

Angina: Pain referred to the heart, usually associated with physical effort. II is due, in most instances, to inadequate blood supply to the heart muscle.

Angiography: The visualization of blood vessels by the use of X-ray and the injection of some form of contrast material.

Ankylosis: Complete or partial loss of motion in a joint; the union of bones forming a joint causing a stiff joint.

Anterior: Posterior: Front to back.

Apposition: The fitting together.

Aphakia: Absence of the lens of the eye.

Aphasia: Loss of power of speech; inability to talk.

Arteriosclerosis or atherosclerosis: So-called "hardening of the arteries." A degenerative condition in which the walls of the arteries lose their elasticity and at times become calcified. As a result, there may be some restriction of blood flow.

Arthrodesis: An operative procedure to eliminate a joint and cause fusion of two adjacent bones.

Arthrography: The visualization of the interior of a joint by use of contrast material and X-ray.

Arthroplasty: An operative procedure to restore motion to a joint.

Arthroscope: A surgical instrument that can be inserted into a joint through a small incision, allowing visualization of the interior of the joint, and allowing surgical procedures of certain types.

Cartilaginous Discs: Plates which act as shock absorbers between the bones of the vertebrae along the spine.

Cerebral Concussion: A minute and diffuse injury to the brain caused by direct or indirect violence. A diagnostic symptom is a loss of consciousness of momentary to prolonged degree. There is often a transient, or permanent, loss of memory for detail preceding the accident for a short time. Symptoms of dizziness or headache, known as the "post-concussion syndrome," may persist for some time, without any objective neurological evidence of damage.

Cervical Spine: The seven upper vertebrae of the spine located in the neck.

Closed Reduction: A reduction accomplished by manipulation or traction without opening the site of the fracture.

Coccyx: The tailbone located in the distal end of the sacrum.

Comminuted Fracture: A fracture in which there are multiple breaks within a given bone resulting in more than two bone pieces or fragments.

Complete Dislocation: A dislocation in which normal contact of one bone with another is entirely lost and one bone is completely separated from any joint contact with the other bone.

Compound Fracture: A fracture in which there is a wound caused either by bone end puncturing the skin or by external force.

Compression Fracture: A fracture in which the bones are violently forced together.

Contact Dermatitis: A skin condition secondary to exposure to some substance for which the patient possesses an allergy or sensitivity.

Coronary Heart Disease: A disease process of the arteries that supply the heart causing chest pain or heart muscle damage, which derives from degenerative changes in the tissue of the artery wall. It is believed to bear a relationship to arteriosclerosis.

CT Scan: "CT stands for "Computerized Tomography." A special X-ray technique which, combined with the computer, allows visualization of the internal parts of the body in better detail than in ordinary X-ray study. At times it is used with injection of contrast materials.

Cystoscope: An instrument to examine the interior of the urinary bladder.

Delayed Union: A union in which the soft union does not harden in the average time but finally solidifies.

Depression Fracture: A fracture in which the bone is driven inward, usually in the skull or face.

Dislocation: Displacement of an organ or joint surfaces.

Distal: Farthest away from the body.

Empyema: A collection of pus within the pleural cavity.

Exploratory: In reference to surgery, means that the diagnosis prior to operation is not too definite, and that actual visualization of pathology is necessary to effect a correct diagnosis.

Fibrous Union: A union in which nature heals the fracture partially but the line and bone cells do not harden resulting in an unsatisfactory healing where the member is not of much use and will not support weight.

Foot-drop: An inability to dorsiflex or raise the foot, which results in a dragging gait, and is indicative of pathology involving the peroneal nerve.

Fracture: An interruption in the normal continuity of a bone.

Functional: In reference to disease, infers that no organic pathology can be found.

Good Firm Body Union: A union in which there is normal healing of a fracture.

Green Stick Fracture: A crack or break not extending completely through the bone.

Herniated Disc: A disc which bulges beyond the edges of the vertebrae and presses against spinal nerves.

Hyperesthesia: Descriptive of an increase in skin sensation.

Hypesthesia (Hypoesthesia): Descriptive of a decrease in skin sensation.

Impacted Fracture: A fracture in which the bones are driven together and held solidly.

Incomplete Dislocation: A dislocation in which the displacement of the bone has only partially occurred with still a portion of one bone end in contact with the other.

Intervertebral Disc: A plate lying between each of the vertebrae consisting of a central core of firm, jelly-like material which acts as a cushion between the vertebrae.

IVP: An abbreviation for "intravenous pyelogram," in which a dye is injected into a vein and the kidney outline is apparent on an X-ray.

Joint-mice: Presence of cartilaginous loose bodies free within a joint cavity.

Laceration: A tear or wound in the soft tissue or skin.

Laminectomy: A surgical procedure removing part, or all, or the lamina of the vertebrae. The lamina is the bony strut that stands between the body and the spinous process on each side and encloses the spinal canal. The term is sometimes used to indicate the operation for removal of a ruptured, or herniated, intervertebral disc.

Lateral: From the side.

Loose Bodies: This term is used interchangeably with joint-mice.

Lumbar Spine: Five lumbar vertebrae located in the lower back.

Lymphadenitis: Inflammation of the lymph glands, secondary to infection.

Mal-Union: A union in which the bone fragments heal in a poor functional position or considerably at variance with the normal bone contour.

Meniscus: A small, crescent-shaped piece of cartilage found at the medial and lateral sides of the knee joint.

Myositis: Inflammation of a muscle.

Neuritis: Inflammation of a nerve.

Neurosis: A condition in which mental, or physical, symptoms may occur secondary to some form of subconscious conflict. Although in most cases no organic pathology Can be found, the condition may progress to the point where physiological changes occur. A not uncommon condition, it is one that should be distinguished from malingering, that is, situations in which the individual consciously manufactures symptoms for monetary or other gain. A "traumatic neurosis" is the development of neurotic symptoms that have been precipitated by an accident or injury.

Non-Union: A union in which no bone structure reforms to span the area between the two bone fragments of the fracture resulting in a condition where only scar tissue holds the bone ends together.

Oblique: At an angle, midway between anterior-posterior and lateral.

Open Reduction: A reduction accomplished through a cutting operation to get the bones back in place which may include wiring, insertion of metal plates, one grafting, or tying the bones together.

Ophthalmology: The field of scientific information concerning the eye.

Organic: In reference to disease, organic means that there is actual tissue pathology as a source for the condition.

Otology: The field of scientific information regarding the ear.

Paracentesis: To remove fluid from within a cavity by means of a large needle.

Paralysis: This may be spastic or flaccid. In the flaccid type there is no voluntary control of the muscles involved, and they are in a completely relaxed condition with absence of muscle tone. In the spastic type there is usually no voluntary control, but the muscles remain in a chronic state of contraction and rigidity.

Paresis: This may refer to softening of the brain, such as may occur with syphilis, with a disturbance of mental function. The term is also frequently used to indicate a muscular weakness of neurologic origin, rather than complete paralysis.

Paresthesia: Abnormal skin sensation in the form of itching, prickling, burning, crawling sensations, etc.

Partial Union: A union in which the new bone does not adequately form to bridge the fracture site.

Passive Motion: Submissive motion or the extent to which the person will allow the member of his body to be moved by the examiner.

Pathological Fracture: A fracture caused by bone weakness.

Phlebitis: Inflammation of a vein.

Pleurisy: Inflammation of the covering membrane of the lungs.

Proximal: Closest to the body.

Psychosis: A severe form of mental illness in which the individual loses contact with reality.

Reduction: The setting of broken bones, or replacing of a dislocated joint, back to the normal condition.

Revision: In reference to surgery, to reconstruct or remodel.

Sacrum: The portion of the spine which joins the whole spine to the pelvis.

Shock: The state of physical collapse.

Simple Fracture: A fracture in which there is a single break in the continuity of the bone.

Spinal Tap: To remove spinal fluid by means of a needle.

Sprain: The result when muscles or ligaments are partially torn, joint fluids may escape, and nerves or blood vessels may be damaged.

Sprain Fracture: A fracture in which the bone is torn off by a tendon or ligament.

Strain: The excessive stretching or overuse of muscles or ligaments.

Tenosynovitis: Inflammation of a tendon and its sheath.

Thoracic Spine: Twelve thoracic vertebrae located in the upper back.

Traction: An arrangement of weights and pulleys to counteract the unsettling pull of muscles attached to a bone.

Transverse Laceration: A tear in which the tissue or skin is torn in a crosswise fashion.

Ultrasound: High-frequency sound waves which may be used for treatment, or diagnosis, of certain types of pathology.

Union: The process of healing of fractured bones.

Varicosity: Refers to varicose veins, meaning abnormal dilatation of certain portions of a vein. This usually leads to failure of valves within the vein and, secondarily, to interference with normal circulation.

Visual Field: An outline of the area of general vision when the eye is kept on a fixed point.

Whiplash: A sprain in the cervico-dorsal area.

APPENDIX 14:
MEANINGS OF ROOTS COMMONLY USED
IN MEDICAL TERMS

Aden	gland	Neph	kidney
Bio	life	Oopher	ovary
Cardi	heart	Ophthalm	eye
Cephal	head	Oss or oste	bone
Chole	bile	Ot	ear
Chondr	cartilage	Ovar	ovary
Cost	rib	Path	disease
Crani	skull	Ped	children
Cyst	sac	Ped	feet
Cyt	cell	Pneum	lung
Derm	skin	Proct	anus
Encephal	brain	Psych	mind
Enter	intestine	Py	pus
Gastr	stomach	Pyel	pelvis
Gynec	woman	Rhin	nose
Hem or hemat	blood	Salping	tube
Hyster	uterus	Septic	poison
Kerat	cornea	Tox	poison
Leuc	white	Trache	trachea
My	muscle		

APPENDIX 15:
MEANINGS OF PREFIXES COMMONLY USED IN MEDICAL TERMS

A or An	absence of	**Hemi**	half
A or Ah	from, away	**Hetero**	other
Ad	to, toward, near	**Homo**	same
Ambi	both	**Hydro**	relating to water
Ante	before	**Hyp**	under or reduced
Anti	against	**Hyper**	above or excessive
Auto	self	**Hypo**	below or deficient
Bi	two	**In**	in
Circum	around	**In**	not
Contra	against, opposed	**Infra**	below
Counter	against	**Inter**	between
Di	two	**Intra**	within
Dis	the opposite of	**Lipo**	relating to fat
Dys	difficult, painful	**Macro**	large
Ecto	outside	**Micro**	small
En	in	**Mon**	single
Eu	well	**Mult**	much or many
Ex or E	from, without	**Odont**	teeth
Exo	outside	**Onych**	nails
Extra	outside	**Osteo**	pertaining to bone
Glosso	relating to the tongue	**Pare**	faulty, related to

Per	throughout	**Scolio**	twisted, bent
Peri	around	**Semi**	half
Phleb	veins	**Sub**	under
Poly	many	**Super**	above
Post	after	**Supra**	above, upon
Pre	before	**Sym or Syn**	with, together
Pro	before	**Trans**	across
Pseud	false	**Tri**	three
Pulmo	relating to the lungs	**Uni**	one
Retro	backward		

APPENDIX 16:
MEANINGS OF SUFFIXES COMMONLY USED IN MEDICAL TERMS

Algia	pain	**Patho**	disease
Asis	condition, state	**Pathy**	disease
Asthenia	weakness	**Penia**	insufficiency
Cele	tumor, hemia	**Pexy**	fixation
Cyte	cell	**Phagia**	eating
Ectasis	dilation	**Phasia**	speech
Ectomy	excision	**Phobia**	fear
Emia	blood	**Plasty**	molding
Esthesia	feeling, sensation	**Pnea**	breathing
Genic	causing	**Ptosis**	falling
Itis	inflammation	**Rhythmia**	rhythm
Logy	science of	**Rrhaphy**	suture of
Oma	tumor	**Uria**	urine
Osis	condition, state		
Ostomy	forming an opening		
Otomy	cutting into		

APPENDIX 17:
SELECTED PROVISIONS OF THE MEDICAL INFORMATION PRIVACY AND SECURITY ACT (S. 573)

SECTION 1. SHORT TITLE; TABLE OF CONTENTS.

(a) SHORT TITLE- This Act may be cited as the 'Medical Information Privacy and Security Act'.

(b) TABLE OF CONTENTS [omitted]

SECTION 2. FINDINGS.

The Congress finds as follows:

(1) Individuals have a right of privacy with respect to their protected health information and records.

(2) With respect to information about medical care and health status, the traditional right of confidentiality (between a health care provider and a patient) is at risk.

(3) An erosion of the right of privacy may reduce the willingness of patients to confide in physicians and other practitioners and may inhibit patients from seeking care.

(4) An individual's privacy right means that the individual's consent is needed to disclose his or her protected health information and that the individual has a right of access to that health information.

(5) Any disclosure of protected health information should be limited to that information or portion of the medical record necessary to fulfill the immediate and specific purpose of the disclosure.

(6) Health research often depends on access to both identifiable and de-identified patient health information and health research is critically important to the health and well-being of all people in the United States.

(7) The Supreme Court found in Jaffee v. Redmond (116 S.Ct. 1923 (1996)) that there is an imperative need for confidence and trust between a psychotherapist and a patient and that such trust can only be established by an assurance of confidentiality. This assurance serves the public interest by facilitating the provision of appropriate treatment for individuals.

(8) Section 264 of the Health Insurance Portability and Accountability Act of 1996 (42 U.S.C. 1320d-2 note) establishes a deadline that Congress enact legislation, before August 21, 1999, to protect the privacy of protected health information.

SECTION 3. PURPOSES.

The purposes of this Act are as follows:

(1) To recognize that there is a right to privacy with respect to health information, including genetic information, and that this right must be protected.

(2) To create incentives to turn protected health information into de-identified health information, where appropriate.

(3) To designate an Office of Health Information Privacy within the Department of Health and Human Services to protect that right of privacy.

(4) To provide individuals with—

(A) access to health information of which they are the subject; and

(B) the opportunity to challenge the accuracy and completeness of such information by being able to file supplements to such information.

(5) To provide individuals with the right to limit the use and disclosure of protected health information.

(6) To establish strong and effective mechanisms to protect against the unauthorized and inappropriate use of protected health information.

(7) To invoke the sweep of congressional powers, including the power to enforce the 14th amendment, to regulate commerce, and to abrogate the immunity of the States under the 11th amendment, in order to address violations of the rights of individuals to privacy, to provide individuals with access to their health information, and to prevent unauthorized use of protected health information that is genetic information.

(8) To establish strong and effective remedies for violations of this Act.

(9) To protect the rights of States.

SECTION 4. DEFINITIONS. [OMITTED]

TITLE I—INDIVIDUALS' RIGHTS

SUBTITLE A—ACCESS TO PROTECTED HEALTH INFORMATION BY SUBJECTS OF THE INFORMATION

SECTION 101. INSPECTION AND COPYING OF PROTECTED HEALTH INFORMATION.

(a) RIGHT OF INDIVIDUAL—

(1) IN GENERAL—A health care provider, health plan, employer, health or life insurer, school, or university, or a person acting as the agent of any such person, shall permit an individual who is the subject of protected health information, or the individual's designee, to inspect and copy protected health information concerning the individual, including records created under sections 102, 112, 202, 203, 208, and 211, that such person maintains.

(2) PROCEDURES AND FEES—A person described in paragraph (1) may set forth appropriate procedures to be followed for inspection and copying under such paragraph and may require an individual to pay fees associated with such inspection and copying in an amount that is not in excess of the actual costs of providing such copying. Such fees may not be assessed where such an assessment would have the effect of inhibiting an individual from gaining access to the information described in paragraph (1).

(b) DEADLINE—A person described in subsection (a)(1) shall comply with a request for inspection or copying of protected health information under this section not later than 15 business days after the date on which the person receives the request.

(c) RULES GOVERNING AGENTS—A person acting as the agent of a person described in subsection (a) shall provide for the inspection and copying of protected health information if—

(1) the protected health information is retained by the agent; and

(2) the agent has been asked by the person involved to fulfill the requirements of this section.

(d) SPECIAL RULE RELATING TO ONGOING CLINICAL TRIALS—With respect to protected health information that is created as part of an individual's participation in an ongoing clinical trial, access to the information shall be provided consistent with the individual's agreement to participate in the clinical trial.

SECTION 102. SUPPLEMENTS TO PROTECTED HEALTH INFORMATION.

(a) IN GENERAL—Not later than 45 days after the date on which a health care provider, health plan, employer, health or life insurer, school, or university, or a person acting as the agent of any such person, receives from an individual a request in writing to supplement protected health information concerning the individual, such person—

(1) shall add the supplement requested to the information;

(2) shall inform the individual that the supplement has been made; and

(3) shall make reasonable efforts to inform any person to whom the portion of the unsupplemented information was previously disclosed, of any substantive supplement that has been made.

(b) REFUSAL TO SUPPLEMENT—If a person described in subsection (a) declines to make the supplement requested under such subsection, the person shall inform the individual in writing of—

(1) the reasons for declining to make the supplement;

(2) any procedures for further review of the declining of such supplement; and

(3) the individual's right to file with the person a concise statement setting forth the requested supplement and the individual's reasons for disagreeing with the declining person and the individual's right to include a copy of this refusal in his or her health record.

(c) STATEMENT OF DISAGREEMENT—If an individual has filed with a person a statement of disagreement under subsection (b)(3), the person, in any subsequent disclosure of the disputed portion of the information—

(1) shall include, at the individual's request, a copy of the individual's statement; and

(2) may include a concise statement of the reasons for not making the requested supplement.

(d) RULES GOVERNING AGENTS—A person acting as the agent of a person described in subsection (a) shall not be required to make a supplement to protected health information, except where—

(1) the protected health information is retained by the agent; and

(2) the agent has been asked by such person to fulfill the requirements of this section.

SECTION 111. ESTABLISHMENT OF SAFEGUARDS.

(a) IN GENERAL—A health care provider, health plan, health oversight agency, public health authority, employer, health researcher, law enforcement official, health or life insurer, school, or university, or a person acting as the agent of any such person, shall establish and maintain appropriate administrative, organizational, technical, and physical safeguards and procedures to ensure the confidentiality, security, accuracy, and integrity of protected health information created, received, obtained, maintained, used, transmitted, or disposed of by such person.

(b) FACTORS TO BE CONSIDERED—The policies and safeguards under subsection (a) shall ensure that—

(1) protected health information is used or disclosed only when necessary;

(2) the categories of personnel who will have access to protected health information are identified; and

(3) the feasibility of limiting access to protected health information is considered.

(c) MODEL GUIDELINES—The Secretary, in consultation with the Director of the Office of Health Information Privacy appointed under section 301, after notice and opportunity for public comment, shall develop and disseminate model guidelines for the establishment of safeguards and procedures for use under this section, such as, where appropriate, individual authentication of uses of computer systems, access controls, audit trails, encryption, physical security, protection of remote access points and protection of external electronic communications, periodic security assessments, incident reports, and sanctions. The director shall update and disseminate the guidelines, as appropriate, to take advantage of new technologies.

TITLE II—RESTRICTIONS ON USE AND DISCLOSURE

SECTION 201. GENERAL RULES REGARDING USE AND DISCLOSURE.

(a) PROHIBITION-

(1) GENERAL RULE—A health care provider, health plan, health oversight agency, public health authority, employer, health researcher, law enforcement official, health or life insurer, school, or university may not disclose or use protected health information except as authorized under this Act.

(2) RULE OF CONSTRUCTION—Disclosure of de-identified health information shall not be construed as a disclosure of protected health information.

(b) SCOPE OF DISCLOSURE-

(1) IN GENERAL—A disclosure of protected health information under this title shall be limited to the minimum amount of information necessary to accomplish the purpose for which the disclosure is made.

(2) DETERMINATION—The determination as to what constitutes the minimum disclosure possible for purposes of paragraph (1) shall be made by a health care provider.

(c) USE OR DISCLOSURE FOR PURPOSE ONLY—A recipient of information pursuant to this title may use or disclose such information solely to carry out the purpose for which the information was disclosed.

(d) NO GENERAL REQUIREMENT TO DISCLOSE—Nothing in this title permitting the disclosure of protected health information shall be construed to require such disclosure.

(e) IDENTIFICATION OF DISCLOSED INFORMATION AS PROTECTED HEALTH INFORMATION—Protected health information disclosed pursuant to this title shall be clearly identified as protected health information that is subject to this Act.

(f) DISCLOSURE BY AGENTS—An agent of a person described in subsection (a)(1), who receives protected health information from the person while acting within the scope of the agency, shall be subject to this title to the same extent as the person and for the duration of the period in which the agent holds the information.

(g) CREATION OF DE-IDENTIFIED INFORMATION—Notwithstanding subsection (c), but subject to the other provisions of this section, a person described in subsection (a)(1) may disclose protected health information to an employee or other agent of the person for purposes of creating de-identified information.

(h) UNAUTHORIZED USE OR DISCLOSURE OF THE DECRYPTION KEY—The unauthorized disclosure of a decryption key shall be deemed to be a disclosure of protected health information. The unauthorized use of a decryption key or de-identified health information in order to identify an individual is deemed to be disclosure of protected health information.

(i) NO WAIVER—Except as provided in this Act, an authorization to disclose personally identifiable health information executed by an individual pursuant to section 202 or 203 shall not be construed as a waiver of any rights that the individual has under other Federal or State laws, the rules of evidence, or common law.

(j) DEFINITIONS [omitted]

SECTION 202. AUTHORIZATIONS FOR DISCLOSURE OF PROTECTED HEALTH INFORMATION FOR TREATMENT AND PAYMENT.

(a) REQUIREMENTS RELATING TO EMPLOYERS, HEALTH PLANS, HEALTH OR LIFE INSURERS, UNINSURED INDIVIDUALS, AND PROVIDERS-

(1) IN GENERAL—To satisfy the requirement under section 201(a)(1), an employer, health plan, health or life insurer, or health care provider that seeks to disclose protected health information in connection with treatment or payment shall obtain an authorization that satisfies the requirements of this section. The authorization may be a single authorization.

(2) EMPLOYERS—Every employer offering a health plan to its employees shall, at the time of an employee's enrollment in the health plan, obtain a signed, written authorization that is a legal, informed authorization that satisfies the requirements of subsection (b) concerning the use and disclosure of protected health information for treatment or payment with respect to each individual who is eligible to receive care under the health plan.

(3) HEALTH PLANS, HEALTH OR LIFE INSURERS—Every health plan or health or life insurer offering enrollment to individual or nonemployer groups shall, at the time of enrollment in the plan or insurance, obtain a signed, written authorization that is a legal, informed authorization that satisfies the requirements of subsection (b) concerning the use and disclosure of protected health information with

respect to each individual who is eligible to receive care under the plan or insurance.

(4) UNINSURED—An originating provider providing health care in other than a network plan setting, or providing health care to an uninsured individual, shall obtain a signed, written authorization that satisfies the requirements of subsection (b) to use protected health information in providing health care or arranging for health care from other providers or seeking payment for the provision of health care services.

(5) PROVIDERS-

(A) IN GENERAL—Every health care provider providing health care to an individual who has not given the appropriate authorization under this section shall, at the time of providing such care, obtain a signed, written authorization that is a legal, informed authorization, that satisfies the requirements of subsection (b), concerning the use and disclosure of protected health information with respect to such individual.

(B) RULE OF CONSTRUCTION—Subparagraph (A) shall not be construed to preclude the provision of health care to an individual who has not given appropriate authorization prior to receipt of such care if—

(i) the health care provider involved determines that such care is essential; and

(ii) the individual can reasonably be expected to sign an authorization for such care when appropriate.

(b) REQUIREMENTS FOR INDIVIDUAL AUTHORIZATION—To satisfy the requirements of this subsection, an authorization to disclose protected health information—

(1) shall identify, by general job description or other functional description, persons authorized to disclose the information;

(2) shall describe the nature of the information to be disclosed;

(3) shall identify, by general job description or other functional description, persons to whom the information is to be disclosed, including individuals employed by, or operating within, an entity to which information is authorized to be disclosed;

(4) shall describe the purpose of the disclosures;

(5) shall permit the executing individual to indicate that a particular individual listed on the authorization is not authorized to receive pro-

tected health information concerning the individual, except as provided for in subsection (c)(3);

(6) shall provide the means by which an individual may indicate that some of the individual's protected health information should be segregated and to what persons such segregated information may be disclosed;

(7) shall be subject to revocation by the individual and indicate that the authorization is valid until revocation by the individual or until an event or date specified; and

(8)(A) shall be—

(i) in writing, dated, and signed by the individual; or

(ii) in electronic form, dated and authenticated by the individual using an authentication method approved by the Secretary; and

(B) shall not have been revoked under subparagraph (A).

(c) LIMITATION ON AUTHORIZATIONS—

(1) IN GENERAL—Subject to paragraphs (2) and (3), a person described in subsection (a) who seeks an authorization under such subsection may not condition the delivery of treatment or payment for services on the receipt of such an authorization.

(2) RIGHT TO REQUIRE SELF PAYMENT—If an individual has refused to provide an authorization for disclosure of administrative billing information to a person and such authorization is necessary for a health care provider to receive payment for services delivered, the health care provider may require the individual to pay from their own funds for the services.

(3) RIGHT OF HEALTH CARE PROVIDER TO REQUIRE AUTHORIZATION FOR TREATMENT PURPOSES—If a health care provider that is seeking an authorization for disclosure of an individual's protected health information believes that the disclosure of such information is necessary so as not to endanger the health or treatment of the individual, the health care provider may condition the provision of services upon the execution of the authorization by the individual.

(d) MODEL AUTHORIZATIONS—The Secretary, in consultation with the Director of the Office of Health Information Privacy, after notice and opportunity for public comment, shall develop and disseminate model written authorizations of the type described in this section and model statements of the limitations on authorizations. Any authorization obtained on a model authorization form under section 202 developed by the Secretary pursuant to the preceding sentence shall be deemed to satisfy the requirements of this section.

(e) SEGREGATION OF FILES—A person described in subsection (a)(1) shall comply, to the maximum extent practicable, with the request of an individual who is the subject of protected health information—

(1) to segregate any type or amount of protected health information, other than administrative billing information, held by the entity; and

(2) to limit the use or disclosure of the segregated health information within the entity to those persons specifically designated by the subject of the protected health information.

(f) REVOCATION OF AUTHORIZATION—

(1) IN GENERAL—An individual may in writing revoke or amend an authorization under this section at any time, unless the disclosure that is the subject of the authorization is required to effectuate payment for health care that has been provided to the individual.

(2) HEALTH PLANS—With respect to a health plan, the authorization of an individual is deemed to be revoked at the time of the cancellation or non-renewal of enrollment in the health plan, except as may be necessary to complete plan administration and payment requirements related to the individual's period of enrollment.

(3) ACTIONS—An individual may not maintain an action against a person for disclosure of personally identifiable health information—

(A) if the disclosure was made based on a good faith reliance on the individual's authorization under this section at the time disclosure was made;

(B) in a case in which the authorization is revoked, if the disclosing person had no actual or constructive notice of the revocation; or

(C) if the disclosure was for the purpose of protecting another individual from imminent physical harm, and is authorized under section 204.

(g) RECORD OF INDIVIDUAL'S AUTHORIZATIONS AND REVOCATIONS—Each person collecting or storing personally identifiable health information shall maintain a record for a period of 7 years of each authorization of an individual and any revocation thereof, and such record shall become part of the personally identifiable health information concerning such individual.

(h) RULE OF CONSTRUCTION—Authorizations for the disclosure of protected health information for treatment or payment shall not authorize the disclosure of such information by an individual with the intent to sell, transfer, or use protected health information for commercial advantage other than the revenues directly derived from the provision of health care to that individual. For such disclosures, a separate authorization that satisfies the requirements of section 203 is required.

SECTION 203. AUTHORIZATIONS FOR DISCLOSURE OF PROTECTED HEALTH INFORMATION OTHER THAN FOR TREATMENT OR PAYMENT.

(a) IN GENERAL—To satisfy the requirement under section 201(a)(1), a health care provider, health plan, health oversight agency, public health authority, employer, health researcher, law enforcement official, health or life insurer, school, or university that seeks to disclose protected health information for a purpose other than treatment or payment may obtain an authorization that satisfies the requirements of subsections (b) and (g) of section 202. Such an authorization under this section shall be separate from an authorization provided under section 202.

(b) LIMITATION ON AUTHORIZATIONS-

(1) IN GENERAL—A person subject to section 202 may not condition the delivery of treatment, or payment for services, on the receipt of an authorization described in this section.

(2) REQUIREMENT FOR SEPARATE AUTHORIZATION—A person subject to section 202 may not disclose protected health information to any employees or agents who are responsible for making employment, work assignment, or other personnel decisions with respect to the subject of the information without a separate authorization permitting such a disclosure.

(c) MODEL AUTHORIZATIONS—The Secretary, in consultation with the Director of the Office of Health Information Privacy, after notice and opportunity for public comment, shall develop and disseminate model written authorizations of the type described in subsection (a). Any authorization obtained on a model authorization form under this section developed by the Secretary shall be deemed to meet the authorization requirements of this section.

(d) REQUIREMENT TO RELEASE PROTECTED HEALTH INFORMATION TO CORONERS AND MEDICAL EXAMINERS—

(1) IN GENERAL—When a Coroner or Medical Examiner or their duly appointed deputies seek protected health information for the purpose of inquiry into and determination of, the cause, manner, and circumstances of an individual's death, the health care provider, health plan,

health oversight agency, public health authority, employer, health researcher, law enforcement officer, health or life insurer, school or university involved shall provide that individual's protected health information to the Coroner or Medical Examiner or to the duly appointed deputies without undue delay.

(2) PRODUCTION OF ADDITIONAL INFORMATION—If a Coroner or Medical Examiner or their duly appointed deputies receives health information from an entity referred to in paragraph (1), such health information shall remain as protected health information unless the health information is attached to or otherwise made a part of a Coroner's or Medical Examiner's official report, in which case it shall no longer be protected.

(3) EXEMPTION—Health information attached to or otherwise made a part of a Coroner's or Medical Examiner's official report, shall be exempt from the provisions of this Act except as provided for in this subsection.

(4) REIMBURSEMENT—A Coroner or Medical Examiner may require a person to reimburse their Office for the reasonable costs associated with such inspection or copying.

(e) REVOCATION OR AMENDMENT OF AUTHORIZATION—An individual may, in writing, revoke or amend an authorization under this section at any time.

(f) ACTIONS—An individual may not maintain an action against a person for disclosure of protected health information—

(1) if the disclosure was made based on a good faith reliance on the individual's authorization under this section at the time disclosure was made;

(2) in a case in which the authorization is revoked, if the disclosing person had no actual or constructive notice of the revocation; or

(3) if the disclosure was for the purpose of protecting another individual from imminent physical harm, and is authorized under section 204.

SECTION 204. EMERGENCY CIRCUMSTANCES.

(a) GENERAL RULE—In the event of a threat of imminent physical or mental harm to the subject of protected health information, any person may, in order to allay or remedy such threat, disclose protected health information about such subject to a health care practitioner, health care facility, law enforcement authority, or emergency medical personnel.

(b) HARM TO OTHERS—Any person may disclose protected health information about the subject of the information where—

(1) such subject has made an identifiable threat of serious injury or death with respect to an identifiable individual or group of individuals;

(2) the subject has the ability to carry out such threat; and

(3) the release of such information is necessary to prevent or significantly reduce the possibility of such threat being carried out.

SECTION 205. PUBLIC HEALTH.

(a) IN GENERAL—A health care provider, health plan, public health authority, employer, health or life insurer, law enforcement official, school, or university may disclose protected health information to a public health authority or other person authorized by public health law when receipt of such information by the authority or other person—

(1) relates directly to a specified public health purpose;

(2) is reasonably likely to achieve such purpose; and

(3) is intended for a purpose that cannot be achieved through the receipt or use of de-identified health information.

(b) PUBLIC HEALTH PURPOSE DEFINED—For purposes of subsection (a), the term 'public health purpose' means a population-based activity or individual effort, authorized by law, aimed at the prevention of injury, disease, or premature mortality, or the promotion of health, in a community, including—

(1) assessing the health needs and status of the community through public health surveillance and epidemiological research;

(2) developing public health policy;

(3) responding to public health needs and emergencies; and

(4) any other activities or efforts authorized by law.

SECTION 206. PROTECTION AND ADVOCACY AGENCIES.

Any person who creates protected health information or receives protected health information under this title may disclose that information to a protection and advocacy agency established under part C of title I of the Developmental Disabilities Assistance and Bill of Rights Act (42 U.S.C. 6041 et seq.) or under the Protection and Advocacy for Mentally Ill Individuals Act of 1986 (42 U.S.C. 10801 et seq.) when such agency can establish that there is probable cause to believe that an individual who is the subject of the protected health information is vulnerable to abuse and neglect by an entity providing health or social services to the individual.

SECTION 207. OVERSIGHT.

(a) IN GENERAL—A health care provider, health plan, employer, law enforcement official, health or life insurer, public health authority, health researcher, school or university may disclose protected health information to a health oversight agency to enable the agency to perform a health oversight function authorized by law, if—

(1) the purpose for which the disclosure is to be made cannot reasonably be accomplished without protected health information;

(2) the purpose for which the disclosure is to be made is of sufficient importance to warrant the effect on, or the risk to, the privacy of the individuals that additional exposure of the information might bring; and

(3) there is a reasonable probability that the purpose of the disclosure will be accomplished.

(b) USE AND MAINTENANCE OF PROTECTED HEALTH INFORMATION—A health oversight agency that receives protected health information under this section—

(1) shall rely upon a method to scramble or otherwise safeguard, to the maximum extent practicable, the identity of the subject of the protected health information in all work papers and all documents summarizing the health oversight activity;

(2) shall maintain in its records only such information about an individual as is relevant and necessary to accomplish the purpose for which the protected health information was obtained;

(3) shall maintain such information securely and limit access to such information to those persons with a legitimate need for access to carry out the purpose for which the records were obtained; and

(4) shall remove or destroy the information that allows subjects of protected health information to be identified at the earliest time at which removal or destruction can be accomplished, consistent with the purpose of the health oversight activity.

(c) USE OF PROTECTED HEALTH INFORMATION IN JUDICIAL PROCEEDINGS—

(1) IN GENERAL—The disclosure and use of protected health information in any judicial, administrative, court, or other public, proceeding or investigation relating to a health oversight activity shall be under-

taken in such a manner as to preserve the confidentiality and privacy of individuals who are the subject of the information, unless disclosure is required by the nature of the proceedings.

(2) LIMITING DISCLOSURE—Whenever disclosure of the identity of the subject of protected health information is required by the nature of the proceedings, or it is impracticable to redact the identity of such individual, the agency shall request that the presiding judicial or administrative officer enter an order limiting the disclosure of the identity of the subject to the extent possible, including the redacting of the protected health information from publicly disclosed or filed pleadings or records.

(d) AUTHORIZATION BY A SUPERVISOR—For purposes of this section, the individual with authority to authorize the oversight function involved shall provide to the disclosing person described in subsection (a) a statement that the protected health information is being sought for a legally authorized oversight function.

(e) USE IN ACTION AGAINST INDIVIDUALS—Protected health information about an individual that is disclosed under this section may not be used in, or disclosed to any person for use in, an administrative, civil, or criminal action or investigation directed against the individual, unless the action or investigation arises out of and is directly related to—

(1) the receipt of health care or payment for health care;

(2) a fraudulent claim related to health; or

(3) oversight of a public health authority or a health researcher.

SECTION 208. DISCLOSURE FOR LAW ENFORCEMENT PURPOSES.

(a) LAW ENFORCEMENT ACCESS TO PROTECTED HEALTH INFORMATION—A health care provider, health researcher, health plan, health oversight agency, employer, health or life insurer, school, university, a person acting as the agent of any such person, or a person who receives protected health information pursuant to section 204, may disclose protected health information to an investigative or law enforcement officer pursuant to a warrant issued under the Federal Rules of Criminal Procedure, an equivalent State warrant, a grand jury subpoena, or a court order under limitations set forth in subsection (b).

(b) REQUIREMENTS FOR COURT ORDERS FOR ACCESS TO PROTECTED HEALTH INFORMATION—A court order for the disclosure of protected health information under subsection (a) may be issued by any court that is a court of competent jurisdiction and shall issue only if the investigative or law enforcement officer submits a written application upon oath or equivalent affirmation demonstrating that there is probable cause to believe that—

(1) the protected health information sought is relevant and material to an ongoing criminal investigation, except in the case of a State government authority, such a court order shall not issue if prohibited by the law of such State;

(2) the investigative or evidentiary needs of the investigative or law enforcement officer cannot reasonably be satisfied by de-identified health information or by any other information; and

(3) the law enforcement need for the information outweighs the privacy interest of the individual to whom the information pertains.

(c) MOTIONS TO QUASH OR MODIFY—A court issuing an order pursuant to this section, on a motion made promptly by the health care provider, health researcher, health plan, health oversight agency, employer, health or life insurer, school, university, a person acting as the agent of any such person, or a person who receives protected health information pursuant to section 204, may quash or modify such order if the court finds that information or records requested are unreasonably voluminous or if compliance with such order otherwise would cause an unreasonable burden on such persons.

(d) NOTICE—

(1) IN GENERAL—Except as provided in paragraph (2), no order for the disclosure of protected health information about an individual may be issued by a court under this section unless prior notice of the application for the order has been served on the individual and the individual has been afforded an opportunity to oppose the issuance of the order.

(2) NOTICE NOT REQUIRED—An order for the disclosure of protected health information about an individual may be issued without prior notice to the individual if the court finds that notice would be impractical because—

(A) the name and address of the individual are unknown; or

(B) notice would risk destruction or unavailability of the evidence.

(e) CONDITIONS—Upon the granting of an order for disclosure of protected health information under this section, the court shall impose appropriate safeguards to ensure the confidentiality of such information and to protect against unauthorized or improper use or disclosure.

(f) LIMITATION ON USE AND DISCLOSURE FOR OTHER LAW ENFORCEMENT INQUIRIES—Protected health information about an individual that is disclosed under this section may not be used in, or disclosed to any person for use in, any administrative, civil, or criminal action or investigation directed against the individual, unless the action or investigation arises out of, or is directly related to, the law enforcement inquiry for which the information was obtained.

(g) DESTRUCTION OR RETURN OF INFORMATION—When the matter or need for which protected health information was disclosed to an investigative or law enforcement officer or grand jury has concluded, including any derivative matters arising from such matter or need, the law enforcement agency or grand jury shall either destroy the protected health information, or return it to the person from whom it was obtained.

(h) REDACTIONS—To the extent practicable, and consistent with the requirements of due process, a law enforcement agency shall redact personally identifying information from protected health information prior to the public disclosure of such protected information in a judicial or administrative proceeding.

(i) EXCEPTION—This section shall not be construed to limit or restrict the ability of law enforcement authorities to gain information while in hot pursuit of a suspect or if other exigent circumstances exist.

SECTION 209. NEXT OF KIN AND DIRECTORY INFORMATION.

(a) NEXT OF KIN—A health care provider, or a person who receives protected health information under section 204, may disclose protected health information about health care services provided to an individual to the individual's next of kin, or to another person whom the individual has identified, if at the time of the treatment of the individual—

(1) the individual—

(A) has been notified of the individual's right to object to such disclosure and the individual has not objected to the disclosure; or

(B) is in a physical or mental condition such that the individual is not capable of objecting, and there are no prior indications that the individual would object; and

(2) the information disclosed relates to health care services currently being provided to that individual.

(b) DIRECTORY INFORMATION—

(1) DISCLOSURE—

(A) IN GENERAL—Except as provided in paragraph (2), with respect to an individual who is admitted as an inpatient to a health care facility, a person described in subsection (a) may disclose information described in subparagraph (B) about the individual to any person if, at the time of the admission, the individual—

(i) has been notified of the individual's right to object and has not objected to the disclosure; or

(ii) is in a physical or mental condition such that the individual is not capable of objecting and there are no prior indications that the individual would object.

(B) INFORMATION—Information described in this subparagraph is information that consists only of 1 or more of the following items:

(i) The name of the individual who is the subject of the information.

(ii) The general health status of the individual, described as critical, poor, fair, stable, or satisfactory or in terms denoting similar conditions.

(iii) The location of the individual within the health care facility to which the individual is admitted.

(2) EXCEPTION—Paragraph (1)(B)(iii) shall not apply if disclosure of the location of the individual would reveal specific information about the physical or mental condition of the individual, unless the individual expressly authorizes such disclosure.

(c) DIRECTORY OR NEXT-OF-KIN INFORMATION—A disclosure may not be made under this section if the disclosing person described in subsection (a) has reason to believe that the disclosure of directory or next-of-kin information could lead to the physical or mental harm of the individual, unless the individual expressly authorizes such disclosure.

SECTION 210. HEALTH RESEARCH [OMITTED]

SECTION 211. JUDICIAL AND ADMINISTRATIVE PURPOSES.

(a) IN GENERAL—A health care provider, health plan, health oversight agency, employer, insurer, health or life insurer, school or university, a person acting as the agent of any such person, or a person who receives protected health information under section 204, may disclose protected health information—

(1) pursuant to the standards and procedures established in the Federal Rules of Civil Procedure or comparable rules of other courts or administrative agencies, in connection with litigation or proceedings to which an individual who is the subject of the information is a party and in which the individual has placed his or her physical or mental condition at issue;

(2) to a court, and to others ordered by the court, if in response to a court order issued by a court of competent jurisdiction in accordance with subsections (b) and (c); or

(3) if necessary to present to a court an application regarding the provision of treatment of an individual or the appointment of a guardian.

(b) COURT ORDERS FOR ACCESS TO PROTECTED HEALTH INFORMATION—A court order for the disclosure of protected health information under subsection (a) may be issued only if the person seeking disclosure submits a written application upon oath or equivalent affirmation demonstrating by clear and convincing evidence that—

(1) the protected health information sought is necessary for the adjudication of a material fact in dispute in a civil proceeding;

(2) the adjudicative need cannot be reasonably satisfied by de-identified health information or by any other information; and

(3) the need for the information outweighs the privacy interest of the individual to whom the information pertains.

(c) NOTICE—

(1) IN GENERAL—Except as provided in paragraph (2), no order for the disclosure of protected health information about an individual may be issued by a court unless notice of the application for the order has been served on the individual and the individual has been afforded an opportunity to oppose the issuance of the order.

(2) NOTICE NOT REQUIRED—An order for the disclosure of protected health information about an individual may be issued without notice to the individual if the court finds, by clear and convincing evidence, that notice would be impractical because—

(A) the name and address of the individual are unknown; or

(B) notice would risk destruction or unavailability of the evidence.

(d) OBLIGATIONS OF RECIPIENT—A person seeking protected health information pursuant to subsection (a)(1)—

(1) shall notify the individual or the individual's attorney of the request for the information;

(2) shall provide the health care provider, health plan, health oversight agency, employer, insurer, health or life insurer, school or university, agent, or other person involved with a signed document attesting—

(A) that the individual has placed his or her physical or mental condition at issue in litigation or proceedings in which the individual is a party; and

(B) the date on which the individual or the individual's attorney was notified under paragraph (1); and

(3) shall not accept any requested protected health information from the health care provider, health plan, health oversight agency, employer, insurer, health or life insurer, school or university, agent, or person until the termination of the 10-day period beginning on the date notice was given under paragraph (1).

SECTION 212. INDIVIDUAL REPRESENTATIVES.

(a) IN GENERAL—Except as provided in subsections (b) and (c), a person who is authorized by law (based on grounds other than an individual's status as a minor), or by an instrument recognized under law, to act as an agent, attorney, proxy, or other legal representative of a individual, may, to the extent so authorized, exercise and discharge the rights of the individual under this Act.

(b) HEALTH CARE POWER OF ATTORNEY—A person who is authorized by law (based on grounds other than being a minor), or by an instrument recognized under law, to make decisions about the provision of health care to an individual who is incapacitated, may exercise and discharge the rights of the individual under this Act to the extent necessary to effectuate the terms or purposes of the grant of authority.

(c) NO COURT DECLARATION—If a physician or other health care provider determines that an individual, who has not been declared to be legally incompetent, suffers from a medical condition that prevents the individual from acting knowingly or effectively on the individual's own behalf, the right of the individual to authorize disclosure under this Act may be exercised and discharged in the best interest of the individual by—

(1) a person described in subsection (b) with respect to the individual;

(2) a person described in subsection (a) with respect to the individual, but only if a person described in paragraph (1) cannot be contacted after a reasonable effort;

(3) the next of kin of the individual, but only if a person described in paragraph (1) or (2) cannot be contacted after a reasonable effort; or

(4) the health care provider, but only if a person described in paragraph (1), (2), or (3) cannot be contacted after a reasonable effort.

(d) RIGHTS OF MINORS-

(1) INDIVIDUALS WHO ARE 18 OR LEGALLY CAPABLE—In the case of an individual—

(A) who is 18 years of age or older, all rights of the individual under this Act shall be exercised by the individual; or

(B) who, acting alone, can obtain a type of health care without violating any applicable law, and who has sought such care, the individual shall exercise all rights of an individual under this Act with respect to protected health information relating to such health care.

(2) INDIVIDUALS UNDER 18—Except as provided in paragraph (1)(B), in the case of an individual who is—

(A) under 14 years of age, all of the individual's rights under this Act shall be exercised through the parent or legal guardian; or

(B) 14 through 17 years of age, the rights of inspection and supplementation, and the right to authorize use and disclosure of protected health information of the individual shall be exercised by the individual, or by the parent or legal guardian of the individual.

(e) DECEASED INDIVIDUALS—

(1) APPLICATION OF ACT—The provisions of this Act shall continue to apply to protected health information concerning a deceased individual.

(2) EXERCISE OF RIGHTS ON BEHALF OF A DECEASED INDIVIDUAL—A person who is authorized by law or by an instrument recognized under law, to act as an executor of the estate of a deceased individual, or otherwise to exercise the rights of the deceased individual, may, to the extent so authorized, exercise and discharge the rights of such deceased individual under this Act. If no such designee has been

authorized, the rights of the deceased individual may be exercised as provided for in subsection (c).

(3) IDENTIFICATION OF DECEASED INDIVIDUAL—A person described in section 209(a) may disclose protected health information if such disclosure is necessary to assist in the identification of a deceased individual.

SECTION 213. PROHIBITION AGAINST RETALIATION.

A health care provider, health researcher, health plan, health oversight agency, employer, health or life insurer, school or university, person acting as an agent of any such person, or person who receives protected health information under section 204 may not adversely affect another person, directly or indirectly, because such person has exercised a right under this Act, disclosed information relating to a possible violation of this Act, or associated with, or assisted, a person in the exercise of a right under this Act.

TITLE III—OFFICE OF HEALTH INFORMATION PRIVACY OF THE DEPARTMENT OF HEALTH AND HUMAN SERVICES

SUBTITLE A—DESIGNATION [OMITTED]

SUBTITLE B—ENFORCEMENT

CHAPTER 1—CRIMINAL PROVISIONS

SECTION 311. WRONGFUL DISCLOSURE OF PROTECTED HEALTH INFORMATION.

(a) IN GENERAL—Part I of title 18, United States Code, is amended by adding at the end the following:

'CHAPTER 124—WRONGFUL DISCLOSURE OF PROTECTED HEALTH INFORMATION

'Sec. 2801. *Wrongful disclosure of protected health information*

'(a) OFFENSE—The penalties described in subsection (b) shall apply to a person that knowingly and intentionally—

'(1) obtains or attempts to obtain protected health information relating to an individual in violation of title II of the Medical Information Privacy and Security Act; or

'(2) discloses or attempts to disclose protected health information to another person in violation of title II of the Medical Information Privacy and Security Act.

'(b) PENALTIES—A person described in subsection (a) shall—

'(1) be fined not more than $50,000, imprisoned not more than 1 year, or both;

'(2) if the offense is committed under false pretenses, be fined not more than $250,000, imprisoned not more than 5 years, or any combination of such penalties; or

'(3) if the offense is committed with the intent to sell, transfer, or use protected health information for commercial advantage, personal gain, or malicious harm, be fined not more than $500,000, imprisoned not more than 10 years, excluded from participation in any Federally funded health care programs, or any combination of such penalties.

'(c) SUBSEQUENT OFFENSES—In the case of a person described in subsection (a), the maximum penalties described in subsection (b) shall be doubled for every subsequent conviction for an offense arising out of a violation or violations related to a set of circumstances that are different from those involved in the previous violation or set of related violations described in such subsection (a).'.

(b) CLERICAL AMENDMENT—The table of chapters for part I of title 18, United States Code, is amended by inserting after the item relating to chapter 123 the following new item:

'2801'.

SECTION 312. DEBARMENT FOR CRIMES.

(a) PURPOSE—The purpose of this section is to promote the prevention and deterrence of instances of intentional criminal actions which violate criminal laws which are designed to protect the privacy of protected health information in a manner consistent with this Act.

(b) DEBARMENT—Not later than 270 days after the date of enactment of this Act, the Attorney General, in consultation with the Secretary, shall promulgate regulations and establish procedures to permit the debarment of health care providers, health researchers, health or life insurers, employers, or schools or universities from receiving benefits under any Federal health programs or other Federal procurement program if the managers or officers of such persons are found guilty of violating section 2801 of title 18, United States Code, have civil penalties imposed against such officers or managers under section 321 in connection with the illegal disclosure of protected health information, or are found guilty of making a false statement or obstructing justice related to attempting to conceal or concealing such illegal disclosure. Such regulations shall take into account the need for continuity of medical care and may provide for a delay of any debarment imposed under this section to take into account the medical needs of patients.

(c) CONSULTATION—Before publishing a proposed rule to implement subsection (b), the Attorney General shall consult with State law enforcement officials, health care providers, patient privacy rights' advocates, and other appropriate persons, to gain additional information regarding the debarment of entities under subsection (b) and the best methods to ensure the continuity of medical care.

(d) REPORT—The Attorney General shall annually prepare and submit to the Committee on the Judiciary of the House of Representatives and the Committee on the Judiciary of the Senate a report concerning the activities and debarment actions taken by the Attorney General under this section.

(e) ASSISTANCE TO PREVENT CRIMINAL VIOLATIONS—The Attorney General, in cooperation with any other appropriate individual, organization, or agency, may provide advice, training, technical assistance, and guidance regarding ways to reduce the incidence of improper disclosure of protected health information.

(f) RELATIONSHIP TO OTHER AUTHORITIES—A debarment imposed under this section shall not reduce or diminish the authority of a Federal, State, or local governmental agency or court to penalize, imprison, fine, suspend, debar, or take other adverse action against a person, in a civil, criminal, or administrative proceeding.

CHAPTER 2—CIVIL SANCTIONS

SECTION 321. CIVIL PENALTY.

(a) VIOLATION—A health care provider, health researcher, health plan, health oversight agency, public health agency, law enforcement agency, employer, health or life insurer, school, or university, or a person acting as the agent of any such person, who the Secretary, in consultation with the Attorney General, determines has substantially and materially failed to comply with this Act shall be subject, in addition to any other penalties that may be prescribed by law—

> (1) in a case in which the violation relates to title I, to a civil penalty of not more than $500 for each such violation, but not to exceed $5000 in the aggregate for multiple violations;

> (2) in a case in which the violation relates to title II, to a civil penalty of not more than $10,000 for each such violation, but not to exceed $50,000 in the aggregate for multiple violations; or

(3) in a case in which the Secretary finds that such violations have occurred with such frequency as to constitute a general business practice, to a civil penalty of not more than $100,000.

(b) PROCEDURES FOR IMPOSITION OF PENALTIES—Section 1128A of the Social Security Act (42 U.S.C. 1320a-7a), other than subsections (a) and (b) and the second sentence of subsection (f) of that section, shall apply to the imposition of a civil, monetary, or exclusionary penalty under this section in the same manner as such provisions apply with respect to the imposition of a penalty under section 1128A of such Act.

SECTION 322. PROCEDURES FOR IMPOSITION OF PENALTIES [OMITTED]

SECTION 323. CIVIL ACTION BY INDIVIDUALS.

(a) IN GENERAL—Any individual whose rights under this Act have been knowingly or negligently violated may bring a civil action to recover—

(1) such preliminary and equitable relief as the court determines to be appropriate; and

(2) the greater of compensatory damages or liquidated damages of $5,000.

(b) PUNITIVE DAMAGES—In any action brought under this section in which the individual has prevailed because of a knowing violation of a provision of this Act, the court may, in addition to any relief awarded under subsection (a), award such punitive damages as may be warranted.

(c) ATTORNEY'S FEES—In the case of a civil action brought under subsection (a) in which the individual has substantially prevailed, the court may assess against the respondent a reasonable attorney's fee and other litigation costs and expenses (including expert fees) reasonably incurred.

(d) LIMITATION—No action may be commenced under this section more than 3 years after the date on which the violation was or should reasonably have been discovered.

(e) AGENCY—A principal is jointly and severally liable with the principal's agent for damages under this section for the actions of the principal's agent acting within the scope of the agency.

(f) ADDITIONAL REMEDIES—The equitable relief or damages that may be available under this section shall be in additional to any other lawful remedy or award available.

TITLE IV—MISCELLANEOUS [OMITTED]

APPENDIX 18:
AGREEMENT FOR MEDICAL RECORDS REVIEW AND OPINION

This Agreement is made and entered into as of [insert date], by and between [Name of Entity Reviewing Medical Records](hereinafter referred to as "the Company") and [Name of Client Requesting Review of Medical Records] (hereinafter referred to as the "Client").

The undersigned Client understands and agrees to the following:

A. *FORMAT OF THE UNBIASED OPINION*

1. In general, the medical doctor's opinion and report in potential medical malpractice cases will attempt to:

a) Discuss the relevant facts of the case based on the medical records received by us, statement of facts, supporting documents and copies of x-rays (if any).

b) Describe the applicable "standards of medical care." In essence, the report will try to describe what should have been done under those circumstances.

c) Specify what doctor, nurse, hospital or other health care providers, if any, departed from the acceptable "standards of care," in the doctor's opinion. The report will disclose (where legible) who did what and how it was not proper care if that is what the doctor finds.

d) Causation: The report will attempt to show how any substandard care, if the doctor believes that occurred, caused or contributed to any damages (such as injuries, further injuries, complications, worsening of the condition, death) as well as any reasonable potential future injuries, if relevant. If the care was acceptable and complications developed, the report will try to explain that in understandable terms.

To select this review and typewritten opinion, initial line 1 at the bottom of this document.

2. In case reviews that involve accidents, injuries, sickness or health problems not related to questions of medical malpractice, we will have the records reviewed for that concern. The report will attempt to explain what may have caused your current condition, made it worse, as well as potential future problems.

To select this review and typewritten opinion, initial line 2 at the bottom of this document.

3. "Second Opinion": An evaluation of the quality of your medical care that you have been receiving or received. This evaluation is not for the purpose of diagnosis, treatment or recommendations for medical care. The goal of this review of your medical records is to assess the quality of the medical care you are receiving or have received.

To select this review and typewritten opinion, initial line 3 at the bottom of this document.

B. *MEDICAL DIRECTORS HIGHLIGHT MOST IMPORTANT FACTS*

As the records are reviewed, sometimes paperclips are placed on the most important pages and the most significant facts are sometimes highlighted. Therefore, we suggest you keep an extra copy of all records and documents submitted to us to have an unmarked copy for future use. Most Clients and attorneys find this highlighting very helpful in correlating the typed medical opinion with the records that were reviewed. We cannot arrange or tell you in advance, whether or not paperclipping and/or highlighting will be used in the review of your records.

C. *OPINION BASED ON THE RECORDS AND INFORMATION RECEIVED*

The medical records review and typewritten opinions are based upon our receipt of your legible (preferably typed) statement of facts, possible questions and concerns and legible medical records. The opinions expressed will be based on the documents received for review. If they are incomplete or illegible, as much of an opinion as is reasonably possible will be prepared. The necessity for review of any missing documents may be discussed where relevant and possible. You will receive a letter from us confirming receipt of your funds and documents. We cannot confirm anything by telephone or email.

D. *ABOUT THE OPINION*

Our Medical Directors typewritten opinions are their personal opinions prepared confidentially for you. We reserve the right to substitute a Medical Expert opinion at no extra charge to you. Their name will not be revealed to you to maintain their confidentiality. Their opinion will be evaluated by one of our Medical Directors prior to its release to you. However, it is possible that through the legal process, the opinion prepared for you may be "discoverable" by the other side. We suggest that this concern be discussed with an attorney prior to sending any records to us for review.

E. *USE OF THE UNBIASED OPINION*

You and any attorney of your choice can use the typewritten unsigned and anonymous opinion for any legal purpose. Often, Clients just need to know what happened for their peace of mind when there is a medical malpractice concern. Some use it to assist their attorney. After our "Second Opinion" for quality of medical care concerns, some Clients seek second opinions by specialists to treat them or change physicians. Your use of our opinion does not obligate us in any way.

F. *COST OF REVIEW AND OPINION*

The minimum fee for the review of all the medical records, enclosed documents, questions and concerns (if any), and preparation of a typewritten opinion by one of our Medical Directors will be [$xxx] for up to [#] pages reviewed. Every page that exceeds [#] will be [$xxx] per-page. A page is one-sided copying of a single 8 1-2 x 11 inch page of a medical record or document per 8 1-2 x 11 inch sheet of copy paper submitted to us for review. We require a cashier's check or money order made out to [Company Name] to accompany this signed Agreement and your medical records. Your name, address and telephone number must accompany all correspondence and payment to our office and be legible.

After complete payment has been received, the average time for review and preparation of your typewritten report takes approximately six to eight weeks, but that is an estimate. As the records are reviewed, we cannot respond to inquiries as to the status of the report. If you need the report in less time, or within a specified amount of time, an additional "rush fee" of [$xxx] must be submitted.

IF WE CANNOT MEET YOUR RUSH DEADLINE, FOR ANY REASON, OUR ONLY LIABILITY IS TO REFUND TO YOU ALL FEES SUBMITTED.

Any follow-up reviews with a typewritten opinion and additional questions to be answered will be done at an hourly rate of [$xxx] and must be pre-paid. We will be bound by our estimate of time necessary to review any additional records and questions submitted after our receipt of the initial set of medical records and questions (if any).

G. *OPINION IN WRITING ONLY*

There will be no telephone or in-person discussion with our Medical Directors or anyone at our firm concerning the written opinion, before, during during or after it is prepared. Any follow up questions or additional material submitted for further review will be attempted to be answered and reviewed at the hourly rate of [$xxx]. We will give you a cost estimate that will be binding on us and must be pre-paid by cashier's check or money order. The usual response time is approximately six weeks, unless an additional "rush charge" of [$xxx] is also submitted to us.

H. *NUMEROUS MEDICAL EXPERTS AVAILABLE*

Should your attorney want or need an opinion by a "Medical Expert" (a specialist who can prepare his or her own opinion and testify in court), our Company has numerous available on our Independent Consulting Staff. We require that all the arrangements and fees for our Company's services and the Medical Expert Consultant's services be coordinated through your attorney.

I. *OTHER DOCTORS MAY OR MAY NOT AGREE WITH OPINION*

We want you to understand that the typewritten opinion you will receive will be based on the records and documents we receive, and the interpretation and expertise of our Medical Directors. Different doctors reviewing the same set of records may come to completely different opinions. We do not guarantee or assure you in any way that other doctors and even the Medical Experts on our Independent Consulting Staff will agree with any or all of the opinions of our Medical Directors. Their work is highly respected, but opinions do vary widely among doctors.

J. *LOSS OR DAMAGE OF MEDICAL RECORDS*

We use UPS and U.S. Postal Service to ship most of our records to and from our Medical Directors and you. We are not responsible for any loss or damage to those documents. For this reason, we also urge you to keep a complete set of all your medical records and documents you send to us. Do not send us any originals of x-rays, sonograms, CAT scans or MRIs. If you feel that they are needed in addition to any x-ray reports that are in the medical records, only send us copies. We will assume that any such x-rays and similar studies that we receive are only copies.

You agree to hold the Company and anyone we send these records to harmless for any loss or damage to anything you send us for review. Do not send us microscopic slides. Only send the pathology reports that are usually contained within the medical records.

K. *NO LEGAL ADVICE*

The medical doctor performing the review of the medical records and preparing a written opinion, and the Company, which processes the records, correspondence and payment, do not practice law. We are not attorneys and cannot and will not give you any legal advice, neither in writing or verbally. Only a licensed attorney can perform this service for you, and only an attorney, not us, can protect your legal rights.

L. *CONSULT AN ATTORNEY TO PROTECT YOUR LEGAL RIGHTS*

The medical doctor and Company urge you to contact an attorney without any delay to determine what legal deadlines are applicable to your potential case, and what steps you must take now, without any delay, to protect all your rights that may be lost by any delay. We cannot advise you as to your legal deadlines in any way. An acceptance of your case for review does not imply any form of legal protection for you, your case and your legal rights. Consult with an attorney before you send us your records.

M. *NO MEDICAL ADVICE*

By accepting your case for review and opinion, we do not accept you or anyone associated with your case as a patient. We do not practice medicine and do not give medical advice. Only a licensed physician in your state who accepts you as a patient and treats you, can give you medical advice, recommend tests, prescribe medications and care, and in any other way, function as your health care provider. We do not.

N. *RESPONSIBILITY FOR SUCCESS OR FAILURE OF CASE*

Our liability is limited only to the fees we receive from you. Whether you win or lose your case, incur additional expenses, or receive less than you expect, has nothing to do with our services or opinions, and you agree to hold the Company harmless for any such liability.

Furthermore, we are not in any way responsible for any effect or change our opinions may have on your health, medical care or related expenses and you agree to hold the Company harmless for any such liability. In addition, we are not responsible for the opinions, qualifications or cooperation of any Medical Expert that we may refer to your attorney or you for their services.

O. *BINDING ARBITRATION*

Should there be any dispute or claim between you and the Company, all parties agree that such dispute or claim shall be settled by mandatory and binding arbitration in accordance with the commercial arbitration rules of the [applicable arbitration association]. The locale of such arbitration shall be [city/state] and any award rendered pursuant to such arbitration may be entered as a judgment in any court of competent jurisdiction in [state]. Such arbitration will be governed by the [applicable statute]. In the event of such arbitration, or litigation to enforce any award entered pursuant to such arbitration, the prevailing party shall be awarded reasonable attorney's fees and costs.

P. *LIMITED LIABILITY*

It is understood that any and all references to "us", "we", "our" or the "Company" in this Agreement refers to [Company Name], its officers, agents and employees, our Medical Directors, and also to consulting Medical Experts. No other representation(s) of any kind, verbal or written, stated or implied, are part of or modify this Agreement in any way. This Agreement is binding on you and all of your heirs, and assigns. IT IS AGREED THAT THE COMPANY'S TOTAL LIABILITY IS LIMITED ONLY TO THE FEES YOU PAID US.

Q. *GOVERNING LAW*

This Agreement shall be governed and interpreted in accordance with the laws of the [state]. All parties irrevocably submit to have any dispute resolved in [city/state] in the appropriate proceeding.

R. *FORMAT SELECTION*

As stated in Section A above, place your initials next to the type of format you are selecting for review and opinion:

1) _____ I want your unbiased typewritten opinion on potential medical malpractice issues.

2) _____ I want your unbiased typewritten opinion concerning the accident, injury, illness or health related matter as the potential cause of my medical problems or condition.

3) _____ I want your unbiased typewritten "Second Opinion" on the quality of medical care I have been receiving or received.

I have read this entire document and have had the opportunity to consult with an attorney, if I chose to do so. I understand and agree to all the terms, conditions and information presented in this document. I am eighteen (18) years of age or older.

I have enclosed a cashier's check or money order for a total of

[$xxx] which includes [$xxx] to cover the regular minimum fee plus [$xxx] to cover any voluminous record charge and rush fee (if applicable), made payable to [Company Name]. Attached or enclosed with this Agreement is a legible statement of facts, questions of concern (if any), and a copy of my medical records.

Date:

Signature Line for Client:

Client's Name:

Client's Address:

Client's Telephone:

Date:

Accepted by:

[Name of Company]

Signature Line for Authorized Signature

Source: Medical Review Foundation, Inc.

APPENDIX 19:
SAMPLE NEW YORK STATE RETAINER AGREEMENT IN A MEDICAL MALPRACTICE CASE

RETAINER AGREEMENT

DATED this 1st day of December, 2001, the undersigned, Mr. John Doe ("Client"), retains and employs Mary Jones, Esq. ("Attorney") as his Attorney to prosecute or adjust a claim for damages arising from *[state details of applicable claims, e.g. personal injury sustained by [name], wrongful death of [name], loss of services of [name], property damage to [specify], etc]* on *[date of loss]* through the negligence of *[name of defendant]* or other responsible persons.

The Client hereby gives Attorney the exclusive right to take all legal steps to enforce this claim through trial and appeal. The attorney shall have the right but not the obligation to represent the client on appeal.

In consideration of the services rendered and to be rendered by Attorney, the undersigned agrees to pay Attorney and Attorney is authorized to retain out of any monies that come into Attorney's hand by reason of the above claim, the following compensation:

(1) 30 percent on the first $250,000 of the sum recovered,

(2) 25 percent on the next $250,000 of the sum recovered,

(3) 20 percent on the next $500,000 of the sum recovered,

(4) 15 percent on the next $250,000 of the sum recovered,

(5) 10 percent on any amount over $1,250,000 of the sum recovered; or

(6) *Insert any other applicable conditions.*

Such percentage shall be computed on the net sum recovered after deducting from the amount recovered expenses and disbursements for expert testimony and investigative or other services properly chargeable to the enforcement of the claim or prosecution of the action.

In computing the fee, the costs as taxed, including interest upon a judgment, shall be deemed part of the amount recovered.

For the following or similar items there shall be no deduction in computing such percentages: liens, assignments or claims in favor of hospitals, for medical care and treatment by doctors and nurses, or self-insurers or insurance carriers.

In the event extraordinary services are required Attorney may apply to the court for greater compensation pursuant to the Special Rules of the Appellate Division regulating the conduct of attorneys.

If the cause of action is settled by Client without the consent of Attorney, Client agrees to pay Attorney the above percentage of the full amount of the settlement for the benefit of Client, to whomever paid or whatever called.

The attorney shall have, in the alternative, the option of seeking compensation on a quantum meruit basis to be determined by the court. In such circumstances the court would determine the fair value of the service.

Attorney shall have, in addition, Attorney's taxable costs and disbursements.

In the event the Client is represented on appeal by another attorney, Attorney shall have the option of seeking compensation on a quantum meruit basis to be determined by the court.

By signing below where indicated, Client acknowledges that he has received a copy of this retainer letter and has read and agreed to its terms and conditions.

ACCEPTED BY: _____

JOHN DOE, CLIENT

The above employment is hereby accepted on the terms stated.

ACCEPTED BY: _____

MARY JONES, ATTORNEY

STATE OF NEW YORK   )

COUNTY OF WESTCHESTER   )

On the 1st day of December, 2001, before me personally came JOHN DOE, known to me to be the same person who executed the foregoing retainer and acknowledged to me that he executed the same.

_____

NOTARY PUBLIC

APPENDIX 20:
STATE STATUTES GOVERNING LIMITS ON ATTORNEY FEES IN MEDICAL MALPRACTICE CASES

JURISDICTION	STATUTE	APPLICABLE PROVISION
Alabama	None	Alabama does not place a cap on attorneys' fees in medical malpractice actions.
Alaska	None	Alaska does not limit the amount an attorney may recover in fees in a medical malpractice action.
Arizona	None	Arizona does not place a limit on the fees recoverable by an attorney in a medical malpractice action.
Arkansas	None	Arkansas does not place a limit on the fees recoverable by an attorney in a medical malpractice action.
California	Cal. Bus. & Prof. Code § 6146	California limits the amount attorneys in a medical malpractice case can collect pursuant to a contingent fee arrangement to 40 percent of the first $50,000, 33 1/3 percent of the next $50,000, 25 percent of the next $500,000, and 15 percent of any amount that exceeds $600,000.
Colorado	None	Colorado does not place a limit on attorneys' fees in a medical malpractice action.

JURISDICTION	STATUTE	APPLICABLE PROVISION
Connecticut	Conn. Gen. Stat. Ann. § 52-251c	An attorney may only receive a contingency fee up to the following amounts: 33 1/3 percent of the first $300,000, 25 percent of the next $300,000, 20 percent of the next $300,000, 15 percent of the next $300,000, and 10 percent of any amount which exceeds $1,200,000.
Delaware	Del. Code Ann. tit. 18, § 6865	Delaware limits the amount attorneys may collect as a contingency fee in connection with medical malpractice claims to 35 percent of the first $100,000 in damages, 25 percent of the next $100,000, and 10 percent of any remaining award.
District of Columbia	None	The District of Columbia does not place a statutory cap on the fees an attorney may recover in a medical malpractice action.
Florida	Fl. Atty. Conduct Reg. 4-1.5(f)(4)(B)	The Supreme Court of Florida has declared that attorneys' fees in excess of the following amounts are presumed unreasonable: (1) In cases that settle before filing an answer or appointing an arbitrator, 33 1/3 percent of any recovery up to $1,000,000, 30 percent of any recovery between $1,000,000 and $2,000,000, and 20 percent of any excess over $2,000,000; (2) In cases that settle subsequently or go to trial, 40 percent of any recovery up to $1,000,000, 30 percent of any recovery between $1,000,000 and $2,000,000, and 20 percent of any excess over $2,000,000; (3) In cases in which liability is admitted and only damages are contested, 33 1/3 percent of any recovery up to $1,000,000, 20 percent of any recovery between $1,000,000 and $2,000,000, and 15 percent of any excess over $2,000,000; (4) In cases that are appealed an extra 5 percent over what is otherwise allowed.
Georgia	None	There is no limitation in Georgia on the amount of fees attorneys can collect in a medical malpractice action. Contingent fee arrangements need not be approved by the court.
Hawaii	Haw. Rev. Stat. § 607-15.5	Hawaii does not limit attorneys' fees in medical malpractice actions; however, fee arrangements must be approved by the court.

JURISDICTION	STATUTE	APPLICABLE PROVISION
Idaho	None	Idaho has no statutory cap on attorneys' fees.
Illinois	735 Ill. Comp. Stat. Ann. § 5/2-1114	Attorney's contingent fee in a medical malpractice case is limited to (a) 33 1/3 percent of the first $150,000 recovered; (b) 25 percent of the next $850,000 recovered; and (c) 20 percent of any amount over $1,000,000.
Indiana	Ind. Code Ann. § 34-18-18-1.	A claimant's attorney may not receive more than fifteen percent of any award from the Patient Compensation Fund.
Iowa	Iowa Code Ann. § 147.138	Iowa does not place a limit on the fees an attorney may recover in a medical malpractice action. However, Iowa courts are charged with the responsibility of determining the reasonableness of fee arrangements between medical malpractice claimants and their counsel.
Kansas	None	There is no Kansas statute limiting attorneys' fees in medical malpractice actions.
Kentucky	None	Kentucky does not limit the amount an attorney can charge a client.
Louisiana	None	Louisiana does not place a limit on the amount of fees a claimant's attorney may receive for services rendered in a medical malpractice action.
Maine	Me. Rev. Stat. Ann. tit. 24, § 2961	Attorney cannot collect contingent fees in excess of 33 1/3 percent of the first $100,000 recovered; 25 percent of the next $1,00,000 recovered; and 20 percent of any amount above $200,000.
Maryland	Md. Code Ann., Cts. & Jud. Proc. § 3-2A-07	When attorneys' fees are in dispute the claimed fees must first be approved by the arbitration panel or court.
Massachusetts	Mass. Ann. Laws ch. 231, § 60I	Attorney fees may not exceed the following limits: (a) 40 percent of the first $150,000 recovered; (b) 33 1/3 percent of the next $150,000 recovered; (c) 30 percent of the next $200,000 recovered; and (d) 25 percent of any amount by which the recovery exceeds $500,000.

JURISDICTION	STATUTE	APPLICABLE PROVISION
Michigan	Mich. Comp. Laws Ann. § 600.919	Compensation of attorneys is left to the express or implied agreement of the parties subject to court rule.
Minnesota	None	Minnesota does not place a limit on attorneys' fees in medical malpractice actions.
Mississippi	None	Mississippi does not place a cap on the amount attorneys can collect in fees.
Missouri	Mo. Ann. Stat. § 484.130	Missouri does not place a limit on the amount of compensation an attorney may receive for services rendered in a medical malpractice action.
Montana	None	There is no Montana statutory provision which limits attorneys' fees in medical malpractice actions.
Nebraska	None	Nebraska does not place a limit on the fees a medical malpractice claimant's attorney may recover for services rendered.
Nevada	None	Nevada does not limit the fees an attorney may collect in a medical malpractice action.
New Hampshire	N.H. Rev. Stat. Ann. § 508:4-e	All fees for actions resulting in a settlement or judgment of $200,000 or more are subject to approval by the court.
New Jersey	N.J. Ct. R. § 1:21-7	Fees may not exceed the following amounts: (a) 33 1/3 percent of the first $500,000; (b) 30 percent of the second $500,000; (c) 25 percent of the third $500,000; (d) 20 percent of the fourth $500,000; and (e) a reasonable amount approved by the court for the excess over $2 million.
New Mexico	None	There is no New Mexico statute limiting attorneys' fees in medical malpractice actions.
New York	N.Y. Jud. Law § 474-a	Attorneys' contingent fees in a medical malpractice action shall not exceed the following schedule: (a) 30 percent of the first $250,000; (b) 25 percent of the next $250,000; (c) 20 percent of the next $500,000; (d) 15 percent of the next $250,000; and (e) 10 percent of any amount over $1,250,000.
North Carolina	None	North Carolina does not limit the fees an attorney may recover in a medical malpractice action.

JURISDICTION	STATUTE	APPLICABLE PROVISION
North Dakota	N.D. Cent. Code § 28-26-01	North Dakota does not place a cap on attorneys' fees.
Ohio	None	Ohio law does not place a limit on the fees a medical malpractice claimant's attorney may receive.
Oklahoma	Okla. Stat. Ann. tit. 5, § 7	Attorneys may lawfully contract for a percentage of the recovery but such percentage may not exceed 50 percent.
Oregon	None	Oregon does not place a cap on the amount attorneys can charge a client.
Pennsylvania	None	Pennsylvania does not place a cap on the amount attorneys can charge a client.
Rhode Island	None	Rhode Island does not place a limit on fees an attorney may recover in a medical malpractice action.
South Carolina	None	South Carolina does not impose a statutory cap on attorneys' fees.
South Dakota	None	South Dakota does not limit the attorneys' fees recoverable in a medical malpractice action.
Tennessee	Tenn. Code Ann. § 29-26- 120	Attorney's compensation may not exceed 33 1/3 percent of all damages awarded to the claimant.
Texas	None	Texas does not place a limit on the amount of attorneys' fees counsel may receive in a medical malpractice action.
Utah	Utah Code Ann. § 78-14-7.5	Attorney may not collect a contingency fee that exceeds one third of the amount recovered.
Vermont	None	Vermont does not place a limit on attorneys' fees in a medical malpractice actions.
Virginia	None	Virginia does not place a cap on attorneys' fees in medical malpractice actions.

JURISDICTION	STATUTE	APPLICABLE PROVISION
Washington	Wash. Rev. Code Ann. § 4.24.005	There is no defined cap for attorneys' fees, however, either party charged with the payment of attorneys' fees in a tort action may petition the court within 45 days of receipt of the final billing for a determination of the reasonableness of that party's attorneys' fees.
West Virginia	None	There is no West Virginia statute which limits the fees an attorney may recover in a medical malpractice action.
Wisconsin	Wis. Stat. Ann. § 655.013	Attorneys' fees in medical malpractice cases are limited to the following: (a) 33 1/3 percent of the first $1,000,000 recovered; (b) 25 percent of the first $1,000,000 recovered if liability was stipulated within 180 days after the complaint was filed and no later than 60 days before the first day of trial; and (c) 20 percent of any amount that exceeds $1,000,000. The court, however, can approve attorneys' fees beyond these limits in exceptional circumstances.
Wyoming	Wyo. Ct. Rules Ann., Contingent Fee R. 5	The following contingent fees are presumed reasonable and not excessive in casualty or wrongful death cases where the total recovery is $1,000,000 or less: (a) 33 1/3 percent if the claim is settled prior to or within 60 days after suit is filed; or (b) 40 percent if the claim is either settled more than 60 days after filing suit or judgment is entered upon a verdict.

APPENDIX 21:
SAMPLE CERTIFICATE OF MERIT

[CAPTION OF CASE]

CERTIFICATE OF MERIT

I am an attorney at law duly licensed to practice in the State of [Name of State], and represent the Plaintiff herein. In compliance with [applicable statute], I hereby certify that I have reviewed the facts of the within case, consulted with at least one physician who is licensed to practice in this state or another state and who I reaasonably believe is knowledgeable in the relevant issues involved in this particular action, and have concluded on the basis of such review and consultation that there is a reasonable basis for the commencement of the within action.

Dated:

Signature Line for Attorney

Attorney Name/Address/Telephone

APPENDIX 22:
SAMPLE MEDICAL RECORDS RELEASE

TO:

Name: _____

Address: _____

RE: _____

Patient Name: _____

Social Security #: _____DOB:_____

Patient Address: _____

Dates of Treatment:_____

Comments: _____

You are hereby authorized to furnish and release to my attorney, [Insert Attorney Name and Address], all of the above-referenced medical records, charts, files, prognoses, reports, and such other information relative to my medical condition and/or treatment at any time provided, to the extent said information is available and within your possession. The foregoing authority shall continue in force until revoked by me, in writing. You are further requested not to disclose information concerning any past or present medical condition to any other person without my express written permission.

Pursuant to [applicable law], we hereby agree to pay up to a maximum of seventy-five (.75) cents per page. Thank you for your cooperation.

Dated:

Authorized Signature

Notary Stamp and Signature

APPENDIX 23:
SAMPLE MEDICAL MALPRACTICE COMPLAINT FOR WRONGFUL DEATH AND NEGLIGENCE AGAINST HOSPITAL

[CAPTION OF CASE]

Plaintiff, by his attorney, complaining of the defendant, alleges upon information and belief as follows:

AS AND FOR A FIRST CAUSE OF ACTION—NEGLIGENCE

1. On the 1st day of June, 2001, the plaintiff, JOHN SMITH (hereinafter referred to as "John Smith" or "administrator"), was duly appointed administrator of the estate of his father, PETER SMITH, deceased, upon the issuance of Limited Letters of Administration by the Surrogate's Court of the County of Nassau, State of New York.

2. Plaintiff, JOHN SMITH, at all times hereinafter mentioned resided at [insert plaintiff's address].

3. Plaintiff's decedent, PETER SMITH (hereinafter referred to as "Mr. Smith," "Father" or "decedent" or "plaintiff"), at all times hereinafter mentioned resided, at [insert decedent's address]

4. Upon information and belief, at all times hereinafter mentioned, the Defendant ANYTOWN CITY HOSPITAL (hereinafter referred to as "Anytown" or "hospital"), was and still is a domestic corporation duly organized and existing under and by virtue of the laws of the State of New York, which operates and maintains a hospital facility, with its principal place of business located at [insert hospital address].

5. Upon information and belief, Defendant ANYTOWN, its agents, servants, and/or employees managed, maintained, operated and were in control of said hospital, which holds itself out as a hospital duly qualified and capable of rendering adequate medical care and treatment to the public, and for such purposes employs doctors, nurses, and other personnel.

6. Upon information and belief, the Defendant ANYTOWN, and its employees, undertook the medical care and treatment of the Plaintiff's decedent, PETER SMITH on January 1, 2000

7. Upon information and belief, the Defendant, ANYTOWN, and its employees, rendered medical treatment to PETER SMITH during the time period of January 1, 2000 until his death on January 5, 2000.

8. The Plaintiff was at all time using due care.

9. The medical care, diagnosis, assessment and treatment rendered by Defendant ANYTOWN and its employees was performed in a negligent and careless manner, as more fully set forth herein and in the following statement of facts, and constitutes professional negligence and malpractice resulting in severe, conscious physical and mental pain and suffering of Plaintiff's decedent, PETER SMITH, prior to death, resulting in his wrongful death on January 5, 2000.

10. The Defendant, ANYTOWN, was careless in its employment and supervision of doctors, nurses, and other medical personnel and employees, causing severe, physical and mental personal injuries and conscious pain and suffering to Plaintiff's decedent resulting in his death on January 5, 2000.

11. Plaintiff alleges the doctrine of respondeat superior.

STATEMENT OF FACTS

12. On January 1, 2000, plaintiff's decedent fell in their home and was taken by ambulance to Anytown City Hospital complaining of neck, back and shoulder pain.

13. The decedent arrived at the emergency room of defendant ANYTOWN at approximately 11:30 p.m. On January 1st, immobilized in a neck brace, and brought to the emergency room.

14. Decedent's family was advised by decedent's employee, an emergency room resident, that after such a fall as the one taken by the decedent, there was always the possibility of a spinal fracture. The family was further advised that a CAT scan of decedent's neck and head would be ordered and performed.

15. Thereafter, the defendant failed to perform the aforementioned CAT scan and/or x-ray of decedent's neck and head. And further failed to On January 5, 2000, the defendant proceeded to discharge the decedent.

16. On the day of discharge, the plaintiff arrived at the hospital to assist the decedent in preparing for discharge.

17. Decedent was not wearing a neck stabilizing brace nor had he had any x-rays or cat scans of his neck despite constant pain.

18. When decedent attempted to get out of the bed, his chin fell to his neck and he lost all feeling in his arms and legs.

19. Plaintiff summoned a nurse to the scene, who assisted plaintiff in returning the decedent to the bed.

20. Plaintiff requested that a neck brace be placed on the decedent and that a CAT scan be taken.

21. Nevertheless, the defendant did not order a CAT scan and did not stabilize plaintiff's neck.

22. Later that same evening, plaintiff received a telephone call from the hospital advising him that the decedent's neck had broken and he had been rendered quadriplegic and would die within several days.

23. On January 5, 2000, decedent died.

24. Defendant, ANYTOWN, its servants and/or employees, were careless and negligent in failing to timely perform a neck CAT scan on their patient, Peter Smith.

25. Defendant, ANYTOWN, its servants and/or employees, were careless and negligent in failing to stabilize the patient's neck.

26. Defendant, ANYTOWN, its servants and/or employees, were careless and negligent in failing to carefully examine the patient;

27. Defendant, ANYTOWN, its servants and/or employees, were careless and negligent in failing to properly diagnose the patient's condition.

28. Defendant, ANYTOWN, its servants and/or employees, were careless and negligent in failing to administer adequate treatment to the patient.

29. Defendant, ANYTOWN, its servants and/or employees, were careless and negligent in failing to properly monitor the patient;

30. Defendant, ANYTOWN, its servants and/or employees, were careless and negligent in failing to recognize spinal injury;

31. Defendant, ANYTOWN, its servants and/or employees, were careless and negligent in failing to adequately treat spinal injury;

32. Defendant, ANYTOWN, its servants and/or employees, were careless and negligent in failing to properly heed the complaints of the patient.

33. Defendant, ANYTOWN, its servants and/or employees, were careless and negligent in failing to comply with the patient and his family's request for a neck brace.

34. Defendant, ANYTOWN, its servants and/or employees, were careless and negligent in failing to comply with the patient and his family's request for a neck CAT scan.

35. Defendant, ANYTOWN, its servants and/or employees, were careless and negligent in failing to carefully handle and otherwise attend to the patient's needs;

36. Defendant, ANYTOWN, its servants and/or employees, were careless and negligent in failing to act with sufficient urgency;

37. By reason of the foregoing, Plaintiff's decedent has been damaged in the sum which exceeds the jurisdiction of any other court which has jurisdiction over this matter.

38. This action falls within the exceptions to CPLR 1602.

AS AND FOR A SECOND CAUSE OF ACTION—GROSS NEGLIGENCE

39. Plaintiff repeats and realleges each and every allegation contained in Paragraphs "1" through "38" of this Complaint, inclusive, as though fully set forth herein.

40. In the medical care, diagnosis, assessment, and treatment rendered by Defendant ANYTOWN CITY HOSPITAL, its servants and/or employees, to the Plaintiff's decedent PETER SMITH, Defendant was sufficiently careless, reckless, wanton and/or malicious so as to constitute gross negligence.

41. In its employment and supervision of doctors, nurses, and other medical personnel, Defendant ANYTOWN CITY HOSPITAL was sufficiently careless, reckless, wanton and/or malicious so as to constitute gross negligence.

42. By reason of the foregoing, the Plaintiff's decedent, PETER SMITH, has been damaged in the sum which exceeds the jurisdiction of any other court which has jurisdiction over this matter.

43. Based on the aforementioned, Plaintiffs are entitled to punitive damages.

AS AND FOR A THIRD CAUSE OF ACTION

44. Plaintiffs repeat and reallege each and every allegation contained in Paragraphs "1" through "43" of this Complaint, inclusive, as though fully set forth herein.

45. Defendant ANYTOWN, its servants and/or employees, prior to the granting or renewing of privileges or employment of Defendant's servants and/or employees, including interns, residents, nurses, doctors and others involved in the Plaintiff's decedent's care, failed to investigate the qualifications, competence, capacity, abilities and capabilities of said servants and/or employees, including but not limited to obtaining the following information: patient grievances, negative health care outcomes, incidents injurious to patients, medical malpractice actions commenced against said persons, including the outcome thereof, any history of association, privilege and/or practice at other institutions, and discontinuation of said association, employment, privilege and/or practice at said institutions, and any pending professional misconduct proceedings in this State or another State, the substance of the allegations in such proceedings and any additional information concerning such proceedings and the findings of the proceedings; and further failed to make sufficient inquiry of the physician, nurse and/or employees and institutions which should and did have information relevant to the capacity, capability, ability and competence of said persons rendering treatment.

46. Had the Defendant made the above-stated inquiry or in the alternative had it reviewed and analyzed the information obtained in a proper manner, privileges and/or employment would not have been granted and/or renewed.

47. By reason of the Defendant ANYTOWN'S failure to meet the aforementioned obligation, plaintiff's decedent was were treated by physicians, nurses and/or other employees who were lacking the requisite skills, abilities, competence and capacity, as a result of which plaintiff's decedent was injured and died.

48. By reason of the foregoing, the Plaintiffs have been damaged in the sum which exceeds the jurisdiction of any other court which has jurisdiction over this matter.

CERTIFICATE OF MERIT

A certificate of merit is annexed hereto.

JURY DEMAND

Plaintiffs demand a jury trial on all issues triable by jury.

RELIEF REQUESTED

WHEREFORE, Plaintiff demands judgment against Defendant ANYTOWN CITY HOSPITAL for each cause of action in an amount as the jury may justly award in accordance with CPLR 3017(c), together with the costs and disbursements of this action.

Dated: Anytown, New York

January 1, 2002

Yours, etc.

[Attorney Name and Address]

VERIFICATION

STATE OF NEW YORK   )

               : ss.

COUNTY OF NASSAU   )

JOHN SMITH, residing at 100 Main Street, Anytown, New York 11530, having been duly sworn, deposes and says that he is a Administrator of the Estate of PETER SMITH, the deceased plaintiff in the above entitled action; that he has read the foregoing Complaint and knows the contents thereof; that the same are true of his own knowledge, except as to matters therein stated to be alleged upon information and belief, and as to those matters he believes it to be true.

[DATE AND TOWN]

       ATTORNEY SIGNATURE LINE

       ATTORNEY NAME/ADDRESS/TELEPHONE

[NOTARY STAMP]

GLOSSARY

Abortion—The premature termination of a pregnancy.

Accrue—To occur or come into existence.

Action at Law—A judicial proceeding whereby one party prosecutes another for a wrong done.

Actionable—Giving rise to a cause of action.

Actionable Negligence—The breach or nonperformance of a legal duty through neglect or carelessness, resulting in damage or injury to another.

Actual Damages—Actual damages are those damages directly referable to the breach or tortious act, and which can be readily proven to have been sustained, and for which the injured party should be compensated as a matter of right.

Ad Damnum Clause—The clause in a complaint which sets forth the amount of damages demanded.

Adjudication—The determination of a controversy and pronouncement of judgment.

Admissible Evidence—Evidence which may be received by a trial court to assist the trier of fact, either the judge or jury, in deciding a dispute.

Adversary—Opponent or litigant in a legal controversy or litigation.

Adversary Proceeding—A proceeding involving a real controversy contested by two opposing parties.

Affirmative Defense—In a pleading, a matter constituting a defense.

Agency—The relationship between a principal and an agent who is employed by the principal, to perform certain acts dealing with third parties.

Agent—One who represents another known as the principal.

Amend—As in a pleading, to make an addition to, or a subtraction from, an already existing pleading.

American Arbitration Association (AAA)—National organization of arbitrators from whose panel arbitrators are selected for labor and civil disputes.

Answer—In a civil proceeding, the principal pleading on the part of the defendant in response to the plaintiff's complaint.

Appeal—Resort to a higher court for the purpose of obtaining a review of a lower court decision.

Appearance—To come into court, personally or through an attorney, after being summoned.

Appellate Court—A court having jurisdiction to review the law as applied to a prior determination of the same case.

Arbitration—The reference of a dispute to an impartial person chosen by the parties to the dispute who agree in advance to abide by the arbitrator's award issued after a hearing at which both parties have an opportunity to be heard.

Arbitration Acts—Federal and state laws which provide for submission of disputes to the process of arbitration.

Arbitration Board—A panel of arbitrators appointed to hear and decide a dispute according to the rules of arbitration.

Arbitration Clause—A clause inserted in a contract providing for compulsory arbitration in case of a dispute as to the rights or liabilities under such contract.

Arbitrator—A private, disinterested person, chosen by the parties to a disputed question, for the purpose of hearing their contention, and awarding judgment to the prevailing party.

Argument—A discourse set forth for the purpose of establishing one's position in a controversy.

Asset—The entirety of a person's property, either real or personal.

Assumption of Risk—The legal doctrine that a plaintiff may not recover for an injury to which he assents.

Attorney In Fact—An attorney-in-fact is an agent or representative of another given authority to act in that person's name and place pursuant to a document called a "power of attorney."

Award—The final and binding decision of an arbitrator, made in writing and enforceable in court under state and federal statutes.

Battery—The unlawful application of force to the person of another.

Bench—The court and the judges composing the court collectively.

Best Evidence Rule—The rule of law which requires the original of a writing, recording or photograph to be produced in order to prove its authenticity.

Bill of Particulars—A request by a party for an amplification of the pleading to which it relates.

Breach of Contract—The failure, without any legal excuse, to perform any promise which forms the whole or the part of a contract.

Breach of Duty—In a general sense, any violation or omission of a legal or moral duty.

Burden of Proof—The duty of a party to substantiate an allegation or issue to convince the trier of fact as to the truth of their claim.

Capacity—Capacity is the legal qualification concerning the ability of one to understand the nature and effects of one's acts.

Caption—The heading of a legal document which contains the name of the court, the index number assigned to the matter, and the names of the parties.

Cause of Action—The factual basis for bringing a lawsuit.

Child Abuse—Any form of cruelty to a child's physical, moral or mental well-being.

Child Protective Agency—A state agency responsible for the investigation of child abuse and neglect reports.

Child Welfare—A generic term which embraces the totality of measures necessary for a child's well being; physical, moral and mental.

Circumstantial Evidence—Indirect evidence by which a principal fact may be inferred.

Civil Action—An action maintained to protect a private, civil right as opposed to a criminal action.

Civil Court—The court designed to resolve disputes arising under the common law and civil statutes.

Civil Law—Law which applies to non-criminal actions.

Claimant—The party who brings the arbitration petition, also known as the plaintiff.

Compensatory Damages—Compensatory damages are those damages directly referable to a breach or tortious act, and which can be readily proven to have been sustained, and for which the injured party should be compensated as a matter of right.

Complaint—In a civil proceeding, the first pleading of the plaintiff setting out the facts on which the claim for relief is based.

Compromise and Settlement—An arrangement arrived at, either in court or out of court, for settling a dispute upon what appears to the parties to be equitable terms.

Compulsory Arbitration—Arbitration which occurs when the consent of one of the parties is enforced by statutory provisions.

Conclusion of Fact—A conclusion reached by natural inference and based solely on the facts presented.

Conclusion of Law—A conclusion reached through the application of rules of law.

Conclusive Evidence—Evidence which is incontrovertible.

Contributory Negligence—The act or omission amounting to want of ordinary care on the part of the complaining party which, concurring with the defendant's negligence, is the proximate cause of his or her injury.

Coroner—The public official whose responsibility it is to investigate the circumstances and causes of deaths which occur within his or her jurisdiction.

Allegation—Statement of the issue that the contributing party is prepared to prove.

Contingency Fee—The fee charged by an attorney, which is dependent upon a successful outcome in the case, and is often agreed to be a percentage of the party's recovery.

Contribution—Sharing of a loss or payment among two or more parties.

Costs—A sum payable by the losing party to the successful party for his or her expenses in prosecuting or defending a case.

Counterclaims—Counterdemands made by a respondent in his or her favor against a claimant. They are not mere answers or denials of the claimant's allegation.

Cross-claim—Claim litigated by co-defendants or co-plaintiffs, against each other, and not against a party on the opposing side of the litigation.

Counterclaims—Counterdemands made by a respondent in his or her favor against a claimant.

Court—The branch of government responsible for the resolution of disputes arising under the laws of the government.

Cross-Examination—The questioning of a witness by someone other than the one who called the witness to the stand concerning matters about which the witness testified during direct examination.

Damages—In general, damages refers to monetary compensation which the law awards to one who has been injured by the actions of another, such as in the case of tortious conduct or breach of contractual obligations.

Defendant—In a civil proceeding, the party responding to the complaint.

Defense—Opposition to the truth or validity of the plaintiff's claims.

Deposition—A method of pretrial discovery which consists of a statement of a witness under oath, taken in question and answer form as it would be in court, with opportunity given to the adversary to be present and cross-examine.

Discovery—Modern pretrial procedure by which one party gains information held by another party.

Duty—The obligation, to which the law will give recognition and effect, to conform to a particular standard of conduct toward another.

Expert Witness—A witness who has special knowledge about a certain subject, upon which he or she will testify, which knowledge is not normally possessed by the average person.

Eyewitness—A person who can testify about a matter because of his or her own presence at the time of the event.

Fact Finder—In a judicial or administrative proceeding, the person, or group of persons, that has the responsibility of determining the acts relevant to decide a controversy.

Fact Finding—A process by which parties present their evidence and make their arguments to a neutral person, who issues a nonbinding report based on the findings, which usually contains a recommendation for settlement.

Finding—Decisions made by the court on issues of fact or law.

Foreseeability—A concept used to limit the liability of a party for the consequences of his acts to consequences that are within the scope of a foreseeable risk.

Fraud—A false representation of a matter of fact, whether by words or by conduct, by false or misleading allegations, or by concealment of that which should have been disclosed, which deceives and is intended to deceive another, and thereby causes injury to that person.

General Damages—General damages are those damages directly referable to the breach or tortious act and which can be readily proven to have been sustained, and for which the injured party should be compensated as a matter of right.

Guardian—A person who is entrusted with the management of the property and/or person of another who is incapable, due to age or incapacity, to administer their own affairs.

Immaterial—Evidence that is not offered to prove a material issue.

Impeach—A showing by means of evidence that the testimony of a witness was unworthy of belief. Also refers to the process of charging a public official with a wrong while still holding office.

Impleader—The process of bringing a third potentially liable party into a pending suit.

Implied Consent—Consent which is manifested by signs, actions or facts, or by inaction or silence, which raises a presumption that consent has been given.

Incapacity—Incapacity is a defense to breach of contract which refers to a lack of legal, physical or intellectual power to enter into a contract.

Infancy—The state of a person who is under the age of legal majority.

Informed Consent—The requirement that a patient be apprised of the nature and risks of a medical procedure before the physician can validly claim exemption from liability for battery, or from responsibility for medical complications.

Injury—Any damage done to another's person, rights, reputation or property.

Intentional Tort—A tort or wrong perpetrated by one who intends to do that which the law has declared wrong, as contrasted with negligence in which the tortfeasor fails to exercise that degree of care in doing what is otherwise permissible.

Interrogatories—A pretrial discovery method whereby written questions are served by one party to the action upon the other, who must reply, in writing, under oath.

Joint and Several—The rights and liabilities shared among a group of people individually and collectively.

Judge—The individual who presides over a court, and whose function it is to determine controversies.

Judgment—A judgment is a final determination by a court of law concerning the rights of the parties to a lawsuit.

Jurisdiction—The power to hear and determine a case.

Jury—A group of individuals summoned to decide the facts in issue in a lawsuit.

Jury Trial—A trial during which the evidence is presented to a jury so that they can determine the issues of fact, and render a verdict based upon the law as it applies to their findings of fact.

Lay Witness—Any witness not testifying as an expert witness.

Legal Capacity—Referring to the legal capacity to sue, it is the requirement that a person bringing the lawsuit have a sound mind, be of lawful age, and be under no restraint or legal disability.

Medical Malpractice—The failure of a physician to exercise that degree of skill and learning commonly applied under all the circumstances in the community by the average prudent reputable professional in the same field.

Minor—A person who has not yet reached the age of legal competence, which is designated as 18 in most states.

Motion—An application to the court requesting an order or ruling in favor of the applicant.

Negligence—The failure to exercise the degree of care which a reasonable person would exercise given the same circumstances.

Negligence Per Se—Conduct, whether of action or omission, which may be declared and treated as negligence without any argument or proof as to the particular surrounding circumstances, because it is contrary to the law.

Nominal Damages—A trivial sum of money which is awarded as recognition that a legal injury was sustained, although slight.

Non Obstante Verdicto (N.O.V.)—Latin for "notwithstanding the verdict." It refers to a judgment of the court which reverses the jury's verdict, based on the judge's determination that the verdict has no basis in law or is unsupported by the facts.

Objection—The process by which it is asserted that a particular question, or piece of evidence, is improper, and it is requested that the court rule upon the objectionable matter.

Pain and Suffering—Refers to damages recoverable against a wrongdoer which include physical or mental suffering.

Parens Patriae—Latin for "parent of his country." Refers to the role of the state as guardian of legally disabled individuals.

Parties—The disputants.

Plaintiff—In a civil proceeding, the one who initially brings the lawsuit.

Pleadings—Refers to plaintiff's complaint which sets forth the facts of the cause of action, and defendant's answer which sets forth the responses and defenses to the allegations contained in the complaint.

Power of Attorney—A legal document authorizing another to act on one's behalf.

Prima Facie Case—A case which is sufficient on its face, being supported by at least the requisite minimum of evidence, and being free from palpable defects.

Proximate Cause—That which, in a natural and continuous sequence, unbroken by any efficient intervening cause, produces injury, and without which the result would not have occurred.

Punitive Damages—Compensation in excess of compensatory damages which serves as a form of punishment to the wrongdoer who has exhibited malicious and willful misconduct.

Question of Fact—The fact in dispute which is the province of the trier of fact, i.e. the judge or jury, to decide.

Question of Law—The question of law which is the province of the judge to decide.

Release—A document signed by one party, releasing claims he or she may have against another party, usually as part of a settlement agreement.

Relief—The remedies afforded a complainant by the court.

Res Ipsa Loquitur—Literally, "the thing speaks for itself." Refers to an evidentiary rule which provides that negligence may be inferred from the fact that an accident occurred when such an occurrence would not ordinarily have happened in the absence of negligence, the cause of the occurrence was within the exclusive control of the defendant, and the plaintiff was in no way at fault.

Respondent—The responding party, also known as the defendant.

Restatement of the Law—A series of volumes authored by the American Law Institute that tell what the law in a general area is, how it is changing, and what direction the authors think this change should take.

Retainer Agreement—A contract between an attorney and the client stating the nature of the services to be rendered and the cost of the litigation.

Service of Process—The delivery of legal court documents, such as a complaint, to the defendant.

Settlement—An agreement by the parties to a dispute on a resolution of the claims, usually requiring some mutual action, such as payment of money in consideration of a release of claims.

Suicide—The deliberate termination of one's existence.

Summons—A mandate requiring the appearance of the defendant in an action under penalty of having judgment entered against him for failure to do so.

Survival Statute—A statute that preserves for a decedent's estate a cause of action for infliction of pain and suffering and related damages suffered up to the moment of death.

Testify—The offering of a statement in a judicial proceeding, under oath and subject to the penalty of perjury.

Testimony—The sworn statement make by a witness in a judicial proceeding.

Tort—A private or civil wrong or injury, other than breach of contract, for which the court will provide a remedy in the form of an action for damages.

Tortfeasor—A wrong-doer.

Tortious Conduct—Wrongful conduct, whether of act or omission, of such a character as to subject the actor to liability under the law of torts.

Transcript—An official and certified copy of what transpired in court or at an out-of-court deposition.

Trial—The judicial procedure whereby disputes are determined based on the presentation of issues of law and fact. Issues of fact are decided by the trier of fact, either the judge or jury, and issues of law are decided by the judge.

Trial Court—The court of original jurisdiction over a particular matter.

Unfit—Incompetent.

Uniform Laws—Laws that have been approved by the Commissioners on Uniform State Laws, and which are proposed to all state legislatures for consideration and adoption.

Venue—The proper place for trial of a lawsuit.

Verdict—The definitive answer given by the jury to the court concerning the matters of fact committed to the jury for their deliberation and determination.

Verification—The confirmation of the authenticity of a document, such as an affidavit.

Vicarious Liability—In tort law, refers to the liability assessed against one party due to the actions of another party.

Voluntary Arbitration—Arbitration which occurs by mutual and free consent of the parties.

Ward—A person over whom a guardian is appointed to manage his or her affairs.

Wrongful Death Statute—A statute that creates a cause of action for any wrongful act, neglect, or default that causes death.

Wrongful Life—In tort law, refers to the birth of a child which should not have occurred for some reason, e.g., the negligent performance of a sterilization procedure.

BIBLIOGRAPHY

The American Board of Medical Specialties (Date Visited: October 2001) <http://www.abms.org/>.

The American Medical Association (Date Visited: October 2001) <http://www.ama-assn.org/>.

The Association for Responsible Medicine (Date Visited: October 2001) <http://www.a-r-m.org/>.

Black's Law Dictionary, Fifth Edition. St. Paul, MN: West Publishing Company, 1979.

Compendium of Selected State Laws Governing Medical Injury Claims. Washington, DC: U.S. Department of Health and Human Services, Agency for Health Care Policy and Research, 1993.

The Federation of State Medical Boards (Date Visited: October 2001) <http://www.fsmb.org/>.

Feuer, William W. *Medical Malpractice Law.* Irvine, CA: LawPrep Press, 1990.

Gifis, Steven H. *Barron's Law Dictionary, Second Edition.* Woodbury, NY: Barron's Educational Series, Inc., 1984.

Health Care Choices (Date Visited: October 2001) <http://www.healthcarechoices.org/>.

The Joint Commission on Accreditation of Healthcare Organizations (JCAHO) (Date Visited: October 2001) <http://www.jcaho.org.>.

Knowx (Date Visited: October 2001)<http://www.knowx.com/>.

King, Jr., Joseph H. *The Law of Medical Malpractice.* St. Paul, MN: West Publishing Co., 1977.

Medical Review Foundation, Inc. (Date Visited: October 2001) <http://www.malpracticeexperts.com/>.

North, Steven E. *Handling Your First Medical Malpractice Case: Fundamentals of Case Management.* New York, NY: Practising Law Institute, 1991.

Schmidt, J.E. *Attorney's Dictionary of Medicine.* New York, NY: Matthew Bender & Company, Inc., 1962.

Schroder, Jack *Identifying Medical Malpractice*. Charlottesville, VA: The Michie Company, 1990.

Smith, James W.*Hospital Liability*. New York, NY: Law Journal Seminars-Press, 1998.